26 WAYS TO USE DRAMA IN TEACHING THE BIBLE

26 WAYS TO USE DRAMA IN TEACHING THE BIBLE

Judy Gattis Smith

A Griggs Educational Resource
Published by
Abingdon Press / Nashville

New text and revisions Copyright © 1988 by Abingdon Press
Original text Copyright © 1975 Griggs Educational Service
(Formerly titled 20 Ways to Use Drama in Teaching the Bible)

93 94 95 96 97 98 99 00 01 02 03—10 9 8 7 6 5 4 3

Library of Congress Cataloging-in-Publication Data

SMITH, JUDY GATTIS, 1933–
    26 ways to use drama in teaching the Bible.
    (A Griggs educational resource)
    Rev. ed. of: 20 ways to use drama in teaching the Bible. 1975.
    1. Drama in Christian education. 2. Bible—Study. I. Smith, Judy Gattis, 1933– .
    20 ways to use drama in teaching the Bible. II. Title.
    III. Title: Twenty-six ways to use drama in teaching the Bible.
            BV1534.4.S64   1988   268'.67   87-33688

ISBN 0-687-42745-2

MANUFACTURED IN THE UNITED STATES OF AMERICA

With Appreciation—
To Pat and Don Griggs

C O N T E N T S

Chapter Five—Acting Under Cover

Chapter Six—Acting Using Electronic Equipment

Chapter Seven—Traditional Dramas in the Church

Chapter Eight—Other Approaches

When first asked to write this book in 1974, I wondered if I could possibly think of twenty different dramatic methods for teaching the Bible. I was convinced of the value of drama as a way to make the Bible come alive, but *twenty* ways? It has been exciting for me to see that not twenty, but twenty plus twenty ways are possible, and in this revision I have added several.

A very old form of drama, the clown, has found its way into the church; a brand new method has emerged with the influx of video cassettes; parts of the body have become actors in their own right; and an old prop has taken on a new importance that makes storytelling a dramatic event. I share these new methods with you with the assurance that as long as there are creative people and our Bible to teach, new forms of drama will continue to emerge.

I challenge you, when you have tried a variety of methods from this book, to develop still other dramatic methods of your own to fit your particular needs and talents. Stay alert to forms of drama developing on the professional stage and on television. Discover old methods that might come full cycle and speak to us with new impact.

Finding ways to make the Bible come alive, to make your classroom exciting, and to involve all your students still calls for the use, in some form or other, of drama.

Judy Gattis Smith, 1987

BIBLICAL SUBJECTS

To decide what type of drama will work best with your particular class, picture it in your mind. How many students are there? Are they active or quiet? Mostly boys or girls? What are their interests? This book is not written to be used straight through. Pick and choose those things that are appropriate for your class. Some general characteristics of certain age groups may be helpful. The suggested methods for young children, with a little adjusting, may be used with older children, and vice versa.

Four and Five Years Old

This age is suited to dramatic play rather than story dramatization. These children like the familiar world, with lots of action. They like things that go, and they love to be on the go themselves. Rhythm plays an important part in their drama; they like to march and skip and hop and run and jump. They are fascinated by sounds and like to imitate. Their interest span is short. The dramas suggested:

Animals Around the Manager
When Jesus Was a Boy
Zacchaeus (first ending)

Six and Seven Years Old

Now the child's world has expanded. These children know more characters through pictures, stories, and plays. Rhythm is still very important. Repetition charms because of their sensitivity to sound. And they still like to imitate. The dramas recommended:

Zacchaeus (second ending)
The Baby Moses Is Saved
When Jesus Was a Boy
Simple Puppet Plays

Eight and Nine Years Old

Children this age have adjusted to their everyday surroundings, and there is increased interest in people and things that are more remote. This age has the ability and enthusiasm to try a number of different types of drama. Those suggested:

The Friend Who Came at Midnight
The Baby Moses Is Saved
Tower of Babel
The Pharisee and the Publican
David and Goliath
Saga of the Bible
String Trick

Ten and Eleven Years Old

By this age the shift is to realistic stories. These children clamor for adventure and excitement and usually are able to read well. Suggestions for dramas:

On the Road to Damascus
Paul in Prison at Philippi
Unforgiving Governor
Boy with the Loaves and Fishes
David and Goliath
Joseph and His Brothers
Saga of the Bible
Video
The Friend Who Came at Midnight
Tower of Babel
Along the Via Dolorosa
Cognitive Learning

Twelve to Fourteen Years Old

A feeling for idealism begins to develop at this age, along with a liking for realism, mystery, and excitement. Recommended for this age group:

Joseph and His Brothers
Beatitudes
Boy with the Loaves and Fishes
Unforgiving Governor
Readings from the Psalms
Tower of Babel
What Is the Kingdom of God Like?
Bridesmaids at a Wedding
On the Road to Damascus
Clowning
Video

Fifteen and Over

The most helpful methods for this age group:

Creative Movement
Readers' Theater
Role-play
Tape-recorder Plays (Creation)
Slide Show
Chancel   Dramas
Simulation Games
Clowning
Foot Drama

On a cold wintery day in December 1223, a poor Italian friar, Francis of Assissi, hurried down the road to the little town of Greccio to preach the Christmas Eve service. As he walked he pondered: What could he say? How could he make the Christmas story come alive for these people? There were few books and fewer people who could read. How could he tell the Christmas story with impact?

As Francis approached Greccio he passed some shepherds huddled around a fire, watching over their sheep. How like the first Christmas! he thought, and an idea began to form in his mind. He would *show* the people the Christmas scene.

When the people arrived at church that Christmas Eve they were amazed. There before a crude manger filled with straw stood a live donkey and an ox, and the carved figures of Mary, Joseph, and shepherds.

With that first manger scene, Francis made the people feel they really had been in Bethlehem on Christmas Eve. Drama had come into the church!

How many church school teachers have felt the same frustration? How can we bring to our students the wonder and delights of the Bible? How can we help them feel with impact the rich content of characters and events? How can we help them experience the lyrical passages, the fantasy, the works of tremendous imaginative power and beauty? How can we teach, through Bible stories, the central themes of the Christian faith? Though the problem of literacy in the middle ages may be different today, the problem of making the Bible come alive is the same Francis faced, and the solution is also the same—drama.

In the past when people have been excited by the Scriptures and able to identify closely with them, there has been a renewal of faith. This renewal and excitement can be experienced in our classrooms when we allow students to participate in noisy, spontaneous, glorious activities that challenge their deepest interests. Though drama can take place in a variety of situations under various conditions, there always should be excitement, a feeling that something vital is happening.

To make the Bible come alive and to make your sessions more exciting and appealing are two good reasons to use drama in your teaching. There is a third reason: The use of drama can give students a sense of adequacy based on self-confidence. Every student has something to offer that can be expressed through drama. What better place than the church to teach the worth of all persons, that each person's contribution is valued and that everyone can express creatively! Particularly in this computer age, it is essential that students become aware of their creative power and be helped to realize that power. Today people spend so much time watching television, sitting in front of a computer, or sitting in a classroom absorbing facts, that they are in danger of losing a chance for self-expression. Drama can overcome this danger.

GETTING STARTED

Having decided that drama just might work, the teacher faces the question, How do I begin? The word *drama* may suggest visions of costumes and properties, elaborate sets, and children with stage fright. Banish that vision! Think of drama in the church school as an "experience," not a "production." Its purpose is to teach, not to direct a performance. In most cases there are no "stars" in our dramas and everyone has an opportunity to participate. Instead of memorized lines there are spontaneous responses; instead of stage fright, creative involvement. Each student's contribution and interpretation is valued. Several of the dramas in this book may be used as productions, but this is never their sole purpose. In fact, a production may be a mistake if it builds in the minds of the students the idea that performance is the main reason for creating plays. Remember, the purpose of drama in the church school is to teach, to sensitize, to foster a creative experience, to play out experiences of the past so as to enlarge the students' understanding of their own life experiences.

Ideally, the church school teacher should be aware when the time is right for creative drama. The teacher should be able to see possibilities in the curriculum that may be lifted out for dramatic interpretation. But this comes with experience.

This book is for the teacher who would like to try some drama in the classroom but lacks the experience to begin confidently. It is for the teacher who is responsible for a program and would like some ideas. From simple pantomime to the symbolic expression of the Creation story—from rhythmic play drama for the very young to a full-scale chancel drama—we suggest a myriad of ways to help bring drama into teaching.

All the playlets in this book have been experienced with actual groups: local church school classes, community vacation church school classes, Conference youth workshops. They have involved persons with a wide range of acting experience—from none to professional training. This book is a result of those experiences. It is an idea book to introduce methods, so that teachers may find those that spark the interest and excitement of their classes.

Not all methods work equally well with all students, but I believe there will be something here that will be just right for your class. With the purchase of this book you obtain the rights to use all the playlets in your class. For maximum benefit, use them as models or as try-out plays. Then you and your class can take it from there.

In some cases the drama is a complete lesson, with follow-up questions and suggested procedures. In others, the emphasis is on teaching the dramatic method, and additional Bible stories that will work well with this method are suggested. In most cases the emphasis is not on biblical *facts*, but on the thoughts and feelings of the people in the Bible. The use of drama helps students realize that biblical characters were real people, with thoughts and feelings much the same as ours. As students experience the physical and emotional aspects of the Bible, they will understand more readily the reasons for and the consequences of the biblical events.

Give it a try, and we think you will join us in saying, "Participate—it's great!"

SOME GUIDELINES FOR TEACHERS

1. Children always prefer to *do* it rather than *talk* about it.

2. Make your instructions clear and vivid, but brief. Always be sure the children understand what is expected of them before you begin the activity.

3. The drama experience you choose should relate directly to the purpose of the lesson.

4. Encourage the children to contribute their own ideas.

5. Most of these methods involve full class participation, but not all children will always participate. Do not force a shy child. A creative teacher can find ways for each child to be involved without being on stage.

6. If equipment is involved, be sure it is in good working order before the session begins.

7. Learn to appreciate noise, but be considerate of other classes by shutting doors.

8. The teacher can work wonders with imagination and a voice that can create mood and atmosphere. Make every effort to cultivate these gifts.

9. Vary your use of drama with other methods of learning. We even grow tired of ice cream if we have it every day.

CHAPTER ONE

Let's look first at the dramatic method *pantomime*. It can be used with any age children or with adults. Pantomime is acting without words, using facial expressions and movements of the body. In this chapter you will find examples of pantomime for several age groups. One story is offered with two endings: the first for children four and five years old, the other for six- and seven-year-olds. Another pantomime is included for children from ten to fourteen years of age.

FIRST WAY . . . ECHO PANTOMIME

Pantomime is an excellent way to begin creative dramatics for the young child, since no words are needed. The four- or five-year-old uses the body naturally to express many thoughts, so pantomime comes easily. Young children do best when they can imitate someone else, so we begin with an echo pantomime. The teacher tells the story with words and actions; the children repeat the teacher's actions and words, adding some of their own if they wish.

Zacchaeus

(BASED ON LUKE 19:1-10)

The purpose of this pantomime is for young children to experience physically the story of Zacchaeus and to let them express themselves through movement.

If this is your class's very first experience of pantomime, you might begin by having the children move expressively to music. Ask them to listen to a piece of music. While they are listening, ask them to move to express how it makes them feel. After this, explain that together, you and they will tell a Bible story with the movement of your bodies. As the story is told, try to move as the people in the story moved.

The Pantomime

There was a man who lived in the days of Jesus, and his name was Zacchaeus.
One morning he got up out of bed
    (everyone stretches)
and put on his robe

(slip arms into imaginary robe)
and sandals,
   (lace up imaginary sandals)
and hurried out of the house.
   (run in place)

He was a little man. (Luke 19:3)

He had heard that Jesus would be passing by that day, and he wanted to see him.
He waited a long time for Jesus to come.
   (shift from one foot to the other impatiently)
As he waited, other people came and pushed him to the back of the crowd.
   (pantomime pushing)
O dear! What could Zacchaeus do? He was very small and could not see over the taller people.
   (stand on tiptoe)
He tried to look around the people on one side,
   (lean to the left)
but he could not see.
   (shake head)
He leaned to the other side,
   (lean to the right)
but he could not see.
   (shake head)
He stood as tall as he could,
   (stretch on tiptoe)
but it was no use.
   (shake head)
Zacchaeus would not be able to see Jesus after all.

Then he had an idea! He would climb a tree. Then he could see over the whole crowd.

He ran to a nearby tree
   (run in place)
and began to climb.
   (climbing motion)
When he got to a good strong limb, he held on tight
   (grasping motion)
and looked down the road.
   (shade eyes with one hand and look)
Sure enough, there was Jesus, coming his way. If only he would pass by this tree!
   Closer and closer Jesus came, until he was right under the tree where Zacchaeus was sitting. Jesus looked up
   (tilt head back and look up)
and called,
   (hand to side of mouth)
"Zacchaeus, hurry and come down, for I will stay at your house today."
   (all children call)
Then Zacchaeus climbed down the tree as fast as he could.
   (pantomime action)
He pushed past the tall people.
   (hands meet and part)
"Jesus is coming to my house," he told them.
   (children repeat)
And he was so happy he skipped round and round, saying, "Jesus is coming to my house."
   (children skip around room)

First Ending—For Very Young Children

All the waiting had been worth it for Zacchaeus. He was more friendly, and happier, from that day on. It was kind of Jesus to go out of his way to pass under the tree where Zacchaeus was sitting and make him happy with a visit.

Question: Who are some people you could make happy with a visit?

Second Ending—For Children Age Six and Seven

Then he ran home
   (run in place)
and prepared supper for Jesus.
   (pantomime placing dish on table)
After they had eaten,
   (pantomime eating)
Zacchaeus said to Jesus, "Lord, half of all that I owe I will give to the poor, and what I have taken from any man I will return to him four times as much."
   Jesus was pleased. He said, "Happiness has come to this house tonight."

Question: If Jesus came to your house, what are some changes you would make in your life?

Possible Uses:
   This echo pantomime can be used with very young children studying "helping others." This may be

all the drama you wish to do at one session. Their interest span is short and it may be best to move to another activity.

First- and second-graders studying "honesty" could use this echo pantomime with the second ending. If they still seem interested and involved after doing the pantomime once, talk over the story with them and then let them play it again on their own.

SECOND WAY . . . PANTOMIME

Pantomime serves a different purpose with older children (10–14). As a story is read aloud, the actors use their entire bodies to experience the story. Relieved of having to say words, they can sharpen their perception of the story and better sense how the character feels. Their imaginations are stimulated.

Pantomime demands individual attention and concentration. The actors can participate in the story in a unique way. No words are spoken. All action takes place in total silence, with the actor's face, hands, and whole body telling the action and expressing the emotions. In the following story the pantomimes are motivated by strong emotions—anger, terror, hate, love.

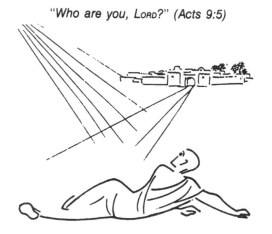

"Who are you, LORD?" (Acts 9:5)

On the Road to Damascus
(BASED ON ACTS 9:1-20)

The purpose of the play *On the Road to Damascus* is to help students identify with Paul at the time of his conversion and try to experience his feelings and the feelings of other persons in the story.

Instructions:

— Decide who the reader will be—a student or the teacher.
— Choose the three main characters: Saul, Stephen, Ananias.
— Divide the rest of the class into three groups to portray the mob, the soldiers, and the Christians.
— Read together Acts 9:1-9.
— Encourage the students to identify the variety of feelings expressed by the characters in the story.
— Give the students a minute or two to decide how they will express their roles through movement.
— Do the pantomime.
— You may wish to do the play several times, with different students taking the main roles.

The Play

My name was Saul of Tarsus.
   (Saul walks onto stage)
I was a devout and educated Jew. I firmly believed that if I obeyed the Jewish law I would please God. After the death of Jesus, his disciples went about saying that Jesus was the Messiah. I had never known Jesus, and I thought his followers were telling lies. I felt it was my duty to fight against those who preached in the name of Jesus. But then a strange thing happened to me. Let me tell you about it. One day I was walking along and came upon a crowd of people.
   (people and Stephen cluster together; Saul walks up to them)
They were gesturing and threatening a man in their midst. I recognized Stephen—a Christian.
   (crowd makes angry faces, wave fists, Stephen cowers)
The crowd became angry. They pushed Stephen. Suddenly one of the group picked up a stone and threw it at him, and soon others joined in the act.
   (pantomime action)
I felt this man was an enemy of God and should be destroyed, but I did not join in the stoning.
   (Saul backs away)
Some of the crowd took off their coats and threw them at my feet.
   (pantomime action)
Stephen fell under the bombardment of rocks. *(Stephen falls)*
I was aware of the depth of his faith even though he was facing death.
I walked away from the crowd, angry and upset.
   (pantomime anger and frustration)
I wanted to destroy all the Christians in Jerusalem and all the towns nearby.
   (crowd and Stephen leave stage)
I put many Christians in prison in Jerusalem, and then I gathered soldiers, so I could go to Damascus and destroy the Christians there also.
   (Saul beckons to soldiers; they join him)
We set off. I was still uttering threats of murder against the disciples of Jesus.
It was a long journey, nearly two hundred miles.
   (pantomime feelings as they walk)
When I was quite near the city, a great light from heaven suddenly shone around me,
   (shield eyes from light)
and I heard a voice saying, "Saul, Saul, why do you persecute me?" I fell to the ground.
   (pantomime action)
I said, "Who are you, Lord?" And the Lord answered, "Get up and go to Damascus, and there you will be told what to do."
   (Saul gets up dazed; soldiers help him)
Suddenly the voice, the light, the whole amazing apparition, was gone. I found I could not see.
   (pantomime blindness)
There was darkness before my eyes, fear in my soul, and unanswered questions in my heart. The soldiers with me had seen the light and heard the voice but could not see anyone, and they were amazed. They led me by the hand into Damascus.
   (soldiers lead Saul to left of stage, then leave)
For three days I was blind, and I ate and drank nothing. Then Ananias, a disciple, came to me and put his hand on me.
   (Ananias enters, pantomimes action)
He said, "Brother Saul, the Lord Jesus who appeared to you on the road has sent me, so that you may

be able to see once more and be filled with the Holy Spirit." Then it seemed as if scales fell from my eyes, and I could see again.

(pantomime action)

I got up and ate and felt stronger.

(pantomime action)

For several days I stayed with the disciples in Damascus.

(Christians enter)

I taught in the synagogues, proclaiming Jesus.

(pantomime preaching to group)

That is how I became one of the witnesses of the Christ. From that day forward I was not Saul, but Paul.

Reflect on the Experience:

A tolerant attitude toward other people can only be achieved through an understanding of the emotional effects their problems have on them. Such an understanding arises through the effort to identify oneself with other persons and understand how they are feeling. Consider the factors that may have led to Paul's conversion. God's Spirit moves into people's lives in many ways, and several factors may have influenced Paul. Most important for understanding his life, however, is the recognition of his conviction that God had confronted him and given him a special task to do.

Discuss with your class how they felt as they acted out this event. Did they actually feel anger and hate and fear? The story is probably familiar to your class. In what ways was it different as they acted it out? What new insights do they have into Paul and his ministry?

The use of pantomime in your classroom need not be limited to these examples. Pantomime can be inserted quickly and easily into any lesson at any time to make a point, to revive class attention, to help students "feel" with a character. Invite students to pantomime when you are finished reading a story by saying something like: "Who wants to pantomime this part of the story we are reading?" "Who can quickly pantomime Paul's escape over the wall of Damascus in a basket?" "What can we do for older retired persons? Show me in pantomime." "Let's pantomime seed time and harvest in Palestine during the time of Ruth. Let's sow the grain, reap with sickles, winnow the chaff from the grain."

Single Bible verses can come alive through pantomime. Here are some examples from the life of Paul:

II Cor. 11:26,27	In my many travels I have been in danger. . . . There has been work and toil; often I have gone without sleep; I have been hungry and thirsty; I have often been without enough food, shelter, or clothing.
Acts 27:43,44	But the army officer wanted to save Paul. . . . He ordered all the men who could swim to jump overboard first and swim ashore; the rest were to follow, holding on to the planks or to some broken pieces of the ship. And this was how we all got safely ashore.
Acts 28:15	The believers in Rome heard about us and came as far as the towns of Market of Appius and Three Inns to meet us. When Paul saw them, he thanked God and was greatly encouraged.

THIRD WAY . . . CREATIVE MOVEMENT

We have used our bodies to help us understand Bible stories by imitation, and by pantomiming actions and feelings. There is another way to use our bodies to help express our feelings about

God—by movement, grace, and physical strength. This is called creative movement, or dance.

Our Spirit has a sense that is satisfied by motion, by doing. We read in Genesis 1:1: "In the beginning God created the heavens and the earth. The earth was without form and void, and darkness was upon the face of the deep; and the Spirit of God was *moving* over the face of the water" (RSV).

Our feelings toward God are more than knowing, and those feelings can be expressed through body movement. The goal in creative movement is not to seek a lovely performance, but to communicate our Christian faith.

For older youths and adults, creative movement is most eloquent when it is more poetic, less specific. Youths and adults can select their own material for creative movement from Bible verses, hymns, prayers. When you select material to interpret, be certain it "speaks" to you. If it does not have meaning for you, your symbolic movements will show that you are only lukewarm. Somehow, you can feel if something is not right. It is difficult to explain, but when what you are doing really has deep meaning and is something you must do, you feel as though you are in another world. You soar! It is worship in a very deep sense.

Everyone can be involved in creative movement. You do not need to be a dancer to enjoy moving. A few simple, yet meaningful examples follow.

What Is the Kingdom of God Like?

The purpose of these experiences is to express in movement our understanding of Jesus' teaching about the kingdom of God. A few students could develop these creative movements as a unique way to present the three Scripture selections. Then the entire class could be involved in working out the interpretation of the remaining three selections.

I—Parable of the Mustard Seed
(BASED ON MATTHEW 13:31-32)

Reader: The kingdom of heaven is like a single mustard seed which a man took and sowed in his field.
(Roll body into a tight ball, drop head forward and bring shoulders forward, making chest hollow until you look like the letter C; drop slowly until sitting on your heels in this position)

Reader: It is the smallest of all seeds, but when it is full grown it is the biggest of shrubs.
(slowly begin to straighten body, lift chest, pull shoulders back, raise head, slowly rise to your feet)

Reader: It becomes like a tree.
(raise arms, focus upward)

Reader: So that birds come and roost in its branches.
(move slowly around trees with flying motions)

II—Parable of the Yeast in the Flour
(BASED ON MATTHEW 13:33)

Reader: The kingdom of heaven is like yeast which a woman took and buried in three measures of flour so that all of it was leavened.
(six class members kneel, head to floor, arms close to body, very close to one another in a circle, heads touching, palms facing outward; slowly all raise arms, focusing upward; members 1, 3, 5 stand slowly, arm to side; they turn to face outward and take a step forward; members 2, 4, 6

CREATIVE MOVEMENT—————————————————————27

repeat those actions; members 1, 3, 5 take two more steps forward, raising arms, focusing up; members 2, 4, 6 repeat those actions; entire group takes four more steps forward, expanding circle)

III—Parable of the Pearl Merchant
(BASED ON MATTHEW 13:45-46)

Reader: The kingdom of heaven is like a merchant in search of fine pearls.
(group in circle; walk counterclockwise, stretching out one arm, then the other; focus on hands)

Reader: Who, on finding one pearl of great value, sold all that he had and bought it.
(touch hands over head; move hands slowly down to side and up again in large circular motions)

Try your own interpretations of Jesus' other parables of the Kingdom. Some to start with: Matt. 13:44; Matt. 13:47-48; Matt. 13:52.

When Jesus Was a Boy

For very young children, creative movement is literal—that is, acting out *words* rather than abstract ideas. Children like to use the fundamental rhythms—run, walk, skip, hop, march, tiptoe, crawl, trot, gallop, run on toes, whirl. Any time you can work these movements into a story or lesson, it takes on more meaning for the young child. Here is an example:

The Story

When Jesus was a little boy he liked to do many of the things you like to do. He would wake up early in the morning and run out to the hills behind his house. Let's pretend we are the little boy Jesus. Run around the room, and I'll tell you what to look for.
(children run around the room; you may use record or piano for background music)

Do you feel the warm sun on your back? Do you feel the dew-wet grass against your feet? Do you feel the cooling breeze? We are tired from running. Lie down full length on the grass.
(children lie down)

Can you smell the flowers all around? Don't they smell good?
Here come some sheep, climbing up the hill. Let's all be sheep. Everyone on all fours. What sounds do sheep make?
(children crawl and "baa")

It is time for Jesus to go back home now. Let's skip on the way home.
(children skip)

Do you see the fields of grain? Do you see the olive trees?
Oh, stop for just a moment. I see a bird in a nest. Everyone tiptoe over to the nest, very quietly.
(children tiptoe)

What kind of bird do you think it is? Do you see the eggs?

Here comes the mother bird. Let's fly like the mother bird.
(children fly)

Jesus was the oldest child in his home. How many of you are the oldest child in your home? Jesus was a happy playmate with his younger brothers and sisters. Listen, they are calling him to come and play. Look, they are playing with a spinning top, just like those you sometimes play with. Can you spin like a top?
(children spin)

Now let's sit down and rest a minute.
(children sit)

Jesus was a happy boy, who played and worked and studied and loved animals and helped others, just as you do. His home was one single room, with stairs outside to a flat roof. At the end of the day he would climb the stairs to the roof. Let's climb.
(children march in place)

There he could feel the cool breeze and look out over the other houses of Nazareth and watch the twinkling stars at night. Sometimes he slept there.
(children curl up to sleep)

Good-night.

CHAPTER TWO

Another simple dramatic method that can make a Bible story come alive is the use of sound. We often read the Bible in the quiet of a church service or a church school when the tone of voice is hushed and solemn. Yet many Bible stories vibrate with noise. In describing the anointing of Solomon as king of Israel, for example, the Bible account says, "They blew the trumpet, and all the people shouted, 'Long live King Solomon!' Then they all followed him back, shouting for joy and playing flutes, making enough noise to shake the ground" (I Kings 1:39-40). How much more exciting to become a part of this exuberantly noisy crowd rather than just read about it.

The next three methods use sound, sound effects, rhythm instruments, and nonsense sounds. These can lead to high volume, and you may understand with new appreciation the words "making enough noise to shake the ground." But the stories should become more vibrant and real.

These methods involve the entire class, and the children become a creative force in telling the story. They become active participants rather than passive listeners.

FOURTH WAY . . . SOUNDS

Very young children are fascinated by sounds, and they love to imitate animals.

Animals Around the Manger
(BASED ON LUKE 2:8-20)

The Christmas story can be made more meaningful to children four and five years old by using this story.

The Story

Come quietly. We are going to tiptoe to the manger and see the baby Jesus. He is asleep, so we must be very quiet. His bed is in a stable and there are friendly animals all around. Look at them. There is a big, warm, brown cow. How does she sound?
(class makes mooing sounds)

Over there is a tiny lamb one of the shepherds brought. He is so soft and fluffy. What kind of sound does the little lamb make?
(class makes baaing sounds)

Look at that shaggy donkey with floppy ears. Does anyone know what kind of sound a donkey makes?

(class makes braying sounds)

Oh, look up there, high in the rafters. There is a dove all nestled down and cooing very softly. Can we make dove sounds?

(class makes cooing sounds)

Do any of you see any other animals?

(children share ideas and make appropriate sounds)

I'm glad the baby Jesus has all those kind, gentle animals to keep him company, aren't you?

The Friend Who Came at Midnight
(BASED ON LUKE 11:5-11)

Most people tend to ignore sounds in self-defense. We are inundated by noise from cars, trucks, planes, factories, sirens, radios. At times it may be necessary to do this to preserve our sanity, but the danger lies in becoming immune to sounds and thereby missing some of the exciting dimensions of life. The ability to interpret sounds is essential if we are to appreciate fully the world around us. This section uses verbal sounds made by the class to bring life to a Bible story.

Jesus did much teaching through stories. Once Jesus told a story about prayer. Ask the children in your class what prayer means to them. When do they pray? If the class does not mention these times, suggest that we pray when we want to share things with God. We pray when we want to thank God. Sometimes we pray for forgiveness when we have done wrong, and sometimes we pray to ask God for help or guidance.

This story is about asking for things. It would be greedy and selfish always to be asking for things. God does not give us everything we ask for, but God does give to us as an expression of love. Because God loves us, it is right to ask for what we need. Jesus said we should go on asking, and he told this story to show what he meant.

Instructions:

—To make the story seem more real, help make the appropriate sounds as you tell the story.
—Divide class into three groups.

    Group 1 - knocking sound (on tables or desks)
    Group 2 - snoring, sleeping sound
    Group 3 - footsteps (running, walking, tiptoeing)

—Practice sounds.
—Decide on a gesture you will make to signal the groups to make their sounds. Practice giving the signal and making the sounds.
—Read the story with responses.

The Story

Ancient people did not keep time as we do today. Instead of clocks, they lived by the sun. They went to bed soon after it was dark and got up when the sun rose. Jewish households divided the night into four parts of three hours each. The evening hours were between 6:00 and 9:00. The time from about 9:00 to 12:00 was called *midnight*. Then came the three hours called *cockcrow*, and at about 3:00 in the morning the hours called *dawn* began.

On the night of our story the sun had gone down and the family was getting ready for bed. Let's hear how it would have sounded.

First there were the running footsteps of the animals as they were herded indoors and settled down for the night.
(group 3)

Then the slower footsteps of the children as they brought out their mats, which had been rolled up and put away in a corner.
(group 3)

Then the big bar of wood was pushed across the door, and soon everyone was fast asleep and all was quiet and still.
(group 2)

Suddenly there came a loud banging at the door.
(group 1)

Who on earth could it be at this hour of the night? There must be something wrong. No one ever disturbed the peace of the night in the little village. The father woke immediately and looked around. The children were still asleep.
(group 2)

"Who is it? What do you want?" asked father. "It is your friend," came the answer. "I am on a journey, and I need food and shelter for the night." Now the whole family was awake and the animals were stirring about.
(group 3)

The friend was welcomed gladly. There were many dangers for a traveler in those days. One could die of thirst in the heat. Robbers hid behind rocks, and wild animals roamed the countryside. Shelter from the bitter cold of the night was important, too. So it was a sacred duty to welcome visitors and give them food and shelter. A traveler could easily die if turned away.

The friend's hands and face and dusty feet were washed, and they all sat down, ready to eat and drink and talk. Then a terrible thing happened. The mother discovered there was no bread in the house. It had all been eaten at supper time. No food for the hungry visitor! This was not just rude and unkind; it was breaking the sacred law! There was only one thing to do—borrow bread from a neighbor. The father tiptoed out of the house.
(group 3)

He wrapped his cloak around him and headed for the neighbor's house.
(group 3)

Next door, the neighbor family was sleeping soundly.
(group 2)

When the father reached the house, he knocked on the door.
(group 1)

Inside, the neighbor was awakened out of a deep sleep. What was that terrible noise? Was it only a dream? The knocking came again.
   (group 1)

Perhaps if he kept quiet, whoever it was would go away. Besides, if he called out, he would wake his family. He pulled his covers over his head. But it was no use. The knocking grew louder and went on.
   (group 1)

Now someone was calling. "Neighbor! Neighbor! Wake up!" The neighbor looked at his sleeping family.
   (group 2)

"Go away," he said.
"But I have a visitor. He has been on the road all day. He needs food," the father called to the neighbor, and then the knocking started again.
   (group 1)

"Everyone here is asleep. Go away."
   (group 2)

But the knocking went on.
   (group 1)

"I must have bread! I'll pay you back tomorrow."
The neighbor did not want to get up at that time of night. He would wake up the whole family to get the bread, as well as disturb the animals, which might mill around, upset, for the rest of the night.
   (group 3)

But the father would not give up. He went on banging on the door, calling out for bread. He would not stop.
   (group 1)

When the neighbor saw it was no use, he awakened his family.
   (group 2)

He had to move all the mats to get to the bread. This disturbed the animals, and they began milling around.
   (group 3)

He took the bar off the door and thrust the loaves into the hands of his friend.
The father thanked him and hurried back to his house, carrying the bread for the needy traveler.
   (group 3)

The father received what he wanted by persisting—by keeping on asking—and there was a happy feast in his house that night.
Next door, the neighbors finally settled back to sleep.
   (group 2)

   When you have finished the play, engage the class in a discussion. Some sample questions you might ask: What are some ways you think God is different from the neighbor who did not like to be wakened in the middle of the night? What ideas do you have about when and where God hears us when we pray? Why do you think the father was so demanding? How do you feel about giving to someone you love? How do you suppose God feels? Do you think all prayers are answered? Why?

FIFTH WAY . . . RHYTHM INSTRUMENTS

Music and rhythm can be exciting additions to a Bible story. In this section we will consider rhythm instruments. Most churches own a set, but if yours does not, simple instructions for making your own are included. Rhythm instruments are a great favorite with young children and can be a unique and fun way to add sound effects to a story. The purpose of the following is to give children a creative experience with sounds and rhythms to intensify the story of Moses in the bulrushes.

Baby Moses Is Saved
(BASED ON EXODUS 2:1-10)

Instructions:

—Gather the following rhythm instruments: horn, sand blocks, drums, sticks, cymbals, gourd rattles.
—If you do not have these instruments available, you can make your own, except for the horn. For sand blocks, use pine blocks covered on the bottom with sheets of 00-grade sandpaper. Attach handles and rub two blocks together. Drums can be metal waste cans turned upside down and hit with a stick. Sticks can be made from two dowels approximately 12" long. Cymbals can be created by fastening large drawer knobs in the centers of two metal piepans. Rattles can be made by placing beans in dried gourds or in other containers that can be sealed.
—Divide the class into five groups and give out the instruments. You will need, in addition, one person to play the horn. Teacher reads the story and directs the groups. In each case (except the horn) the children will play three beats on their instruments. The **boldface type** indicates where the children are to play.

The Story

Long ago in the land of Egypt, there lived a powerful Pharaoh. In the same land, there was a small nation of Hebrew people called the children of Israel. One day Pharaoh walked out of his great palace and made an announcement.

(*horn*) **Da dum da dum**—"All the people of Israel shall be my slaves," he said. And so it was. All became the slaves of Pharaoh. From morning until evening, the children of Israel toiled in hard, back-breaking labor.

(*sand blocks*) **Scrape, scrape, scrape** went their feet across the sand as they pulled the heavy loads.

(*drums*) **March, march, march** went their feet as they dragged the heavy building blocks.

(*sticks*) **Stamp, stamp, stamp**—they worked in the valleys stamping clay.

(*cymbals*) **Crash, crash, crash**—they worked in the hills cutting rocks.

(*rattles*) **Snap, snap, snap** went the whip of the overseer as it cracked upon their backs. They worked without water, without resting, without stopping for breath, and they slaved until they died. "Nothing could be worse than this!" they cried. But things did become worse. The people of Israel continued to multiply and grow restless, and the Pharaoh became afraid of them. And so again he walked out of his great palace and made an announcement.

(horn) **Da dum da dum**—"All the little boys of the children of Israel must die. Every male child that is born to them must be cast into the river." These were indeed bad and bitter days for the children of Israel.

(drums) **March, march, march**—the soldiers clomped through the streets looking for Israelite babies.

(sticks) **Knock, knock, knock**—they beat upon the doors.

(rattles) **Rattle, rattle, rattle**—they sneaked around walls and peeked through cracks.

(cymbals) **Crash, crash, crash**—they came into the rooms and broke things as they searched.

(sand blocks) **Crunch, crunch, crunch**—the Israelites sneaked away, hiding their babies. In one Israelite home, a beautiful baby boy with large, dark eyes was born. "What will become of you?" his mother cried. "God have mercy on this child." For three months the baby was hidden away, and then the mother had an idea.

(sand blocks) **Crunch, crunch, crunch**—the baby's mother and sister tiptoed through the sand, gathering soft bulrushes.

(rattles) **Weave, weave, weave**—the mother and sister wove a small basket from the reeds.

(sticks) **Pat, pat, pat**—they covered the outside with pitch and the inside with clay.

(drums) **Hammer, hammer, hammer**—they stopped up all the holes and cracks. Then they put in a small blanket spread with fragrant myrtle leaves. The basket was completed. When dawn came, the mother gently placed the baby in the basket and put the basket into the river among the reeds under the branches of a willow.

(sticks) **Tap, tap, tap**—the baby's sister, Miriam, gently pushed the basket through the water, then huddled close by to watch.

(cymbals) **Crash, crash, crash**—went the armor of the soldiers as they marched by the river.

(rattles) **Shake, shake, shake**—the reeds quivered in the wind as they kept their precious secret. Ripples lapped against the basket boat. Silvery fish swam by. A monkey chattered in the distance.

(sand blocks) **Scrape, scrape, scrape**—the basket boat gently bobbed against the shore. Now sounds were heard coming toward the river bank.

(sticks) **Tap, tap, tap**—came the sound of many dainty footsteps.

(sand blocks) **Swish, swish, swish**—came the sound of papyrus fans carried by many maidens.

(cymbals) **Clang, clang, clang**—came the sound of heavy jewelry. The Pharaoh's daughter and her handmaids were coming to the river for their noonday bath.

(drums) **Pound, pound, pound**—went the heart of the baby's sister as the group drew closer and closer.

(rattles) **Shake, shake, shake**—the reeds shook as the sister peeped through for a better look. The Pharaoh's daughter stopped at the water's edge. What did she see? Was that a basket rocking gently on the waves? Quickly, she sent one of her maidens for it. And there inside was the beautiful baby with the large, dark eyes.

The baby's sister held her breath. What would happen? The Princess lifted the baby out of the basket and loved him. Miriam jumped from her hiding place and offered to bring a nurse for the baby. And guess who she brought? The baby's own mother!

The Pharaoh's daughter declared she would raise the baby as her own and call him Moses because, she said, "I pulled him out of the water."

And when Moses became a man, he saved his people from slavery and led them out of Egypt, just as the Bible tells us.

(play a marching song: children play instruments and march around the room)

Follow Up:

After using the story as an example, the children will be able to create their own story with rhythm. Have an assortment of instruments available. After reading a Bible story, let the children decide what they will add in the way of sound effects. Instruments can be used to imitate galloping horses, ticking clocks, running water, marching soldiers, and many other sounds.

Your class might enjoy a study of early musical instruments referred to in the Bible. Have them look up the following references to discover instruments used in various ways:

Joshua 6:4 (trumpets from rams' horns)
I Samuel 10:5 (lute, harp, fife, drum)
I Chronicles 15:28 (horns, trumpets, cymbals, lutes, harps)
Daniel 3:5 (horn, pipe, zither, triangle, dulcimer)

SIXTH WAY . . . GIBBERISH

Another fun method of using sounds in acting is gibberish. Gibberish is simply the substituting of no-symbol sounds for recognizable words; it is a vocal utterance that accompanies an action. Gibberish has the inflection, expression, and tone of regular speech, but uses made-up words. Actors use this method to free themselves from dependency on words to express meaning. For students of the Bible, it can give a joyful new experience of a number of Bible stories.

The Tower of Babel
(BASED ON GENESIS 11:1-9)

The purpose of this experience is to help children communicate with pitch, pace, and emphasis, rather than with literal words, and to experience the story of the Tower of Babel in a new way.

The teacher should illustrate what gibberish is before using it in a story. For example, while holding the palm of the hand up to pantomime "stop," utter a gibberish word ("ballarah" or whatever you like). The class will understand what is being communicated. With gestures and gibberish, ask a student to open a window. Have the students turn to their neighbors and carry on conversations as if speaking in an unknown language. They should converse as though making perfect sense. Encourage the students to make as many different sounds as possible. Try to help the students feel relaxed and free in doing the exercise. Gibberish will be easier for some than fpr others. Do not make an issue of this. Accept each child's contribution.

—Explain that you will use gibberish to experience a Bible story. Divide the class into four groups, with at least three persons in each group.

Group 1 - workmen
Group 2 - teachers and students
Group 3 - shopkeepers and street vendors
Group 4 - king and soldiers

—Tell the following story, based on Genesis 11:1-9 and Hebrew myths.

The Story

Once, on the banks of the Euphrates River, there was a great city called Babel. Although a large number of people lived in this city, they all spoke the same language.

This rich and powerful city was ruled over by a king. Though the Bible story does not name the king, legend says that his name was Nimrod.

Nimrod was a proud and haughty king. To show his power he decided to build a great tower, the like of which had never before been seen. The people of Babel were as conceited and presumptuous as their king, and they thought this was a great idea; so a multitude of workmen started to build the tower.

With a base as large as the city, the tower reached 5,000 feet into the air. But the king and the people were not pleased. "Make it higher!" they demanded.

So the workmen added more bricks and stones—layer upon layer—until it was 10,000 feet tall. Surely a tower such as this never had been seen before. But still the king and the people were not pleased.

In their overreaching pride, they shouted, "Build this tower until the top reaches heaven. Let us become equal with God!"

But God, seeing the impossible ambitions of the people, suddenly caused their language to become confused, and the people could no longer understand one another. Everything they said sounded like gibberish.

What would have happened in the city of Babel then?

Assignments:

Hand out the following assignments to each group. Allow them a few minutes to work out their scenes.

Assignment for Group 1—Workmen
You are working on the great tower when this confusion occurs. Immediately, everything goes wrong. A bricklayer asks for a brick and is given stones, or clay, or whatever you wish. Everyone misunderstands everyone else. Finally all the workmen walk off the job. Decide who you will be, and show us this scene in gibberish and action.

Assignment for Group 2—Students and Teacher
You are in a classroom when this confusion occurs. Immediately, everything goes wrong. The teacher gives an instruction that no one understands. The students try to do as they are told. Finally

they all run home. Choose one person to be the teacher; the rest will be students. Show us this scene in gibberish and action.

Assignment for Group 3—Shopkeepers and Street Vendors

You are busy in the marketplace selling your wares when this confusion occurs. Immediately, everything goes wrong. People buy the wrong things, pay the wrong prices. Finally the merchants close the shops. Decide who you will be—shoppers or sellers. Show us this scene in gibberish and action.

Assignment for Group 4—King and Soldiers

The king is in his palace surrounded by soldiers when the confusion occurs. Immediately, everything goes wrong. The king gives an order but no one understands. The soldiers rush about in all directions. Choose someone to be king; the rest will be soldiers. Show us this scene in gibberish and action.

Skits:

When the groups present their skits there will be noise and confusion, but the scenes should have shape and not get out of hand.

The teacher may conclude by saying something like: "Now we can understand better what confusion there must have been. There could be no learning, no working together, no buying and selling—only chaos. The Bible story ends by saying that the people who understood each other formed groups and moved away. Soon the entire population was scattered over the face of the earth. In this way God confused the languages of humankind and divided one people into many nations. And we are still divided by language and race unless God's love brings us together."

Follow Up:

Talk about the book of Genesis. How did we come to have these stories? Why were they told from generation to generation and finally written into our Bible? Research ziggurats—towers built by the ancient Babylonians for religious ceremonies. How might these have influenced the tellers of the Babel story? In what very important way did the Hebrews change the legends of the ancient world? Have the students work individually or in pairs on original stories to explain why there are different nations and different languages on earth. Lead the students to identify current examples of the ways some people today try to make themselves equal with God. Make a list of all the things that go wrong when people do not understand one another. Create another gibberish story. (The Pentecost story would be a good one.)

C H A P T E R   T H R E E

We have seen how Bible stories can be interpreted with pantomime and movement, and we have used sounds to create atmosphere and rhythm. But some portions of the Bible can be most dramatically presented with words alone. This section looks at various methods of reading in unison for dramatic presentation.

SEVENTH WAY . . . CHORAL READING

Choral reading is reading or reciting in unison under the direction of a leader. It can offer a new way to tell a story or give new interpretation to Psalms or other Bible passages. It has the advantage of involving the entire class, regardless of space or class size, and it emphasizes group, rather than individual contribution.

In choral reading we do not use our bodies to act, but attempt to create drama by the blending of words and sentences much as an orchestra does. Voices can be divided into groups: boys and girls, high and low, light and dark, solo and chorus, or any way you like.

Choral reading can be used for performance (as in the pageant in chapter 8) or just as a way to study a Bible story (as in the following).

The Unforgiving Governor
(BASED ON MATTHEW 18:21-35)

Since this story may be familiar, choral reading can present it in a fresh way for your students. Emphasize the creation of feelings and pace with words for maximum learning. Consider this story as a way to present the Scripture lesson in a worship service, as well as in classroom settings.

Instructions:

—Read the entire choral reading to get a feel for the pace. At what points will it go fast? Where slow? Where loud? Where soft?
—Allow time for everyone in the class to read it silently. Until one understands the selection, one cannot interpret it.
—Define any words the students do not understand and work on pronunciations that are unclear.
—Assign the parts:

Solo 1, Solo 2, Emperor, Governor; divide the remainder of the class into Chorus 1 and Chorus 2.

—Rehearse the reading. Direct the students, to help them with pace. Encourage them to begin together and speak at the same rate of speed.

The Reading

Solo 1	Once Peter asked Jesus this question:
Solo 2	"How often should I go on forgiving my brother?"
Solo 1	and Jesus answered by telling a story.
Chorus 1	There once was a mighty emperor
Chorus 2	with a kingdom so vast,
Chorus 1	so big,
Chorus 2	so far-reaching
Chorus 1	that the emperor had to choose servants to help him govern.
Chorus 2	And governors to rule over each part of his great kingdom.
Solo 2	What were these governors supposed to do?
Chorus 1	Keep the people loyal.
Chorus 2	See that everyone obeyed the law.
Chorus 1	Keep peace.
Chorus 2	And—
Solo 2	Yes?
All	(*with emphasis*) And collect the taxes.
Chorus 1	Over the years, the emperor grew lazy.
Chorus 2	He let the governors take over.
Chorus 1	And he did not worry about loyalty,
Chorus 2	or laws,
Chorus 1	or peace,

All	or taxes!
Solo 1	And then suddenly it happened.
Chorus 1	Every governor received a royal command.
Chorus 2	He was ordered to come to the capital city at once.
All	And bring the taxes.
Chorus 1	How they hurried!
Chorus 2	How they scurried!
Chorus 1	Making plans.
Chorus 2	Packing bags.
Chorus 1	*(slowly)* But one governor was very sad.
Chorus 2	He dreaded coming.
Chorus 1	For he had stolen from the emperor.
Solo 2	What, stolen money from the emperor?
Chorus 1	Stolen money from the emperor.
Chorus 2	*(softly)* Stolen money from the emperor.
Chorus 1	And bought himself a fine house.
Chorus 2	And lots of land.
Chorus 1	Each year he had collected taxes.
Chorus 2	But he had not sent the money to the emperor.
Solo 2	And now, would the emperor know?
Chorus 1	The emperor would know.
Chorus 2	*(softly)* The emperor would know.
Chorus 1	And the governor would lose his power.
Chorus 2	And lose his wealth.

Chorus 1	And lose his land.
Chorus 2	And maybe—his life.
Chorus 1	At last the awful day came.
Chorus 2	The emperor sat on his throne.
Chorus 1	All the courtiers gathered around him.
Chorus 2	And the governors came in.
Chorus 1	One by one.
Chorus 2	*(softer)* One by one.
Chorus 1	Then came the governor who had been dishonest,
Chorus 2	and the court officials read out his debt.
Chorus 1	It was huge!
Chorus 2	Enormous!
Chorus 1	Impossible to repay!
Chorus 2	And the people who heard were shocked.
Solo 2	He owes 10,000 talents?
Chorus 1	He owes 10,000 talents.
Chorus 2	*(softly)* He owes 10,000 talents!
Chorus 1	And the room grew quiet
Chorus 2	as everyone waited
Chorus 1	to hear the awful punishment.
Chorus 2	The emperor was furious!
Emperor	You wicked scoundrel! You have been cheating me for years! You owe me 10,000 talents! You and your wife and children will be sold as slaves. Your house and your land and everything you possess will be sold.
Chorus 1	The governor shook with terror.

Chorus 2	He trembled with fright.
Chorus 1	He threw himself on the floor.
Chorus 2	He groveled at the emperor's feet.
Chorus 1	He wept.
Chorus 2	He wailed.
Chorus 1	He moaned.
Chorus 2	He groaned.
All	He cried and cried!
Chorus 1	*(slowly)* And the emperor began to feel pity.
Chorus 2	He was sorry for the man.
All	And he forgave him!
Chorus 1	The huge debt—
Chorus 2	every part of it—
Chorus 1	all was forgotten.
Chorus 2	And he left the palace a free man.
Chorus 1	Everything was forgiven.
Chorus 2	*(softly)* Everything was forgiven.
Solo 1	But the story does not end here. There is more.
Chorus 1	The governor left the palace.
Chorus 2	Still trembling.
Chorus 1	But then—he began to forget.
Chorus 2	He forgot the emperor's kindness.
Chorus 1	He forgot the emperor's forgiveness.
Chorus 2	And he forgot to be grateful.

Solo 2	He forgot all that was forgiven him?
Chorus 1	He forgot it all.
Chorus 2	(softly) He forgot it all.
Chorus 1	Then the governor caught sight of a man from the land he ruled over.
Chorus 2	He was a very poor man.
Chorus 1	And he owed the governor a small sum of money.
Chorus 2	The governor rushed at him
Chorus 1	and grabbed him by the collar
Chorus 2	and demanded his money.
Governor	You swine! Give me the money you owe me or I'll send you to prison! You know I can. And you will stay there until the debt is paid. And you will die there if you don't pay me!
Chorus 1	The poor man shook with terror.
Chorus 2	He trembled with fear.
Chorus 1	A hundred dinars was a lot of money
Chorus 2	for a poor peasant.
Chorus 1	He threw himself on the ground.
Chorus 2	He groveled at the governor's feet.
Chorus 1	He wept.
Chorus 2	He wailed.
Chorus 1	He moaned.
Chorus 2	He groaned.
All	He cried and cried!
Chorus 1	But the governor had no pity on the man.

Chorus 2	He showed him no mercy.
Chorus 1	He had him dragged off to prison.
Solo 2	The governor would not forgive him?
Chorus 1	The governor would not forgive him.
Chorus 2	*(softly)* The governor would not forgive him.
Chorus 1	A crowd began to gather.
Chorus 2	They watched it all.
Chorus 1	They talked to one another.
Chorus 2	They told their friends.
Chorus 1	The story spread and spread.
Chorus 2	Until at last—
Chorus 1	it reached the emperor.
Chorus 2	He immediately sent for the governor.
Emperor	I forgave you your huge debt when you pleaded with me. But you could not forgive that man his little debt when he pleaded with you. Very well. You have chosen your own punishment. I will treat you exactly as you treated him. I will send you to prison, just as you sent him. You will stay there until you have repaid every penny of your debt.
Chorus 1	It was no use to plead now.
Chorus 2	No use to cry.
Chorus 1	The governor had had his chance.
Chorus 2	He was sentenced to the fate he had chosen.
Solo 1	And Jesus told Peter that we must go on forgiving others without limit.
Chorus 1	For we are like the governor.
Chorus 2	And God is like the emperor.
Chorus 1	We owe a huge debt we can never repay.
Chorus 2	God gives us everything.
Solo 2	What is the answer to Peter's question?

Chorus 1   We must forgive each other endlessly.

Chorus 2   *(softly)* We must forgive each other endlessly.

Follow Up:

After the reading, engage the students in discussing their reactions to the story. Some questions you might ask:

1. What were some of your feelings as you read the story?
2. What are some factors that make it easy to forgive someone? What are some that make it hard?
3. Do you think there is anything God could never forgive? Why?

EIGHTH WAY . . . OTHER READING DRAMAS

Psalms are the poetry of the Bible and are meant to be read. Because the sound of the words has as much appeal as the content and mood, they can be meaningful for your class to read and speak.

Following is a variety of ways, in addition to choral reading, to make these hymns of the Hebrew people come alive. These are such easy extensions of traditional reading-aloud activities that any teacher can feel secure in doing them.

Antiphonal Reading

Antiphonal, from the Greek *antiphona* (sounding in response), is defined as "read by two groups alternately." This is an ancient art, evidences of which have been found in the religious ceremonies and festivals of primitive peoples. It was used in Old Testament times and was an important element in early Greek drama. Many of the psalms can be read effectively antiphonally. Ask the class to imagine two groups of Hebrew people standing outdoors in Old Testament times, each on a small rise or hill, facing each other. Shouted, almost chanted, the words of one group cross the dividing valley to be answered by the group on the opposite hill.

Psalm 100 (RSV)

Group 1   Make a joyful noise to the Lord, all the lands!
                 Serve the Lord with gladness! Come into his presence with singing.

Group 2   Know that the Lord is God!
                 It is he that made us, and we are his;
                 we are his people, and the sheep of his pasture.

Group 1   Enter his gates with thanksgiving,
                 and his courts with praise!
                 Give thanks to him, bless his name!

Group 2   For the Lord is good;
                 his steadfast love endures forever,
                 and his faithfulness to all generations.

Cumulative Reading

Use this when you have eight or more students. Begin with soft voices and add volume and depth with stronger voices, building through the entire psalm in crescendo to a loud, glorious climax.

Psalm 150 (RSV)

Reader 1	Praise the LORD!
Readers 1 and 2	Praise God in his sanctuary;
Readers 1, 2, 3	praise him in his mighty firmament!
Readers 1, 2, 3, 4	Praise him for his mighty deeds;
Readers 1, 2, 3, 4, 5	praise him according to his exceeding greatness!
Readers 1, 2, 3, 4, 5, 6	Praise him with trumpet sound; praise him with lute and harp!
Readers 1, 2, 3, 4, 5, 6, 7	Praise him with timbrel and dance; praise him with strings and pipe!
Readers 1, 2, 3, 4, 5, 6, 7, 8	Praise him with sounding cymbals; praise him with loud clashing cymbals!
Readers 1, 2, 3, 4, 5, 6, 7, 8, 9	Let everything that breathes praise the LORD!
All	Praise the LORD!

Line-around Reading

Have twelve students stand in a circle. Each is given one line to read. Reader 1 begins, and the psalm continues around the group. The lovely words should flow like a wave or a current of electricity. This also can be done with six students: Reader 1 reads line 7; Reader 2 reads line 8, and so on.

This psalm is thought to have grown out of the occasion when David brought the Ark of the Covenant to Jerusalem. The class may wish to pantomime this action as they read.

Psalm 24:7-10 (RSV)

Reader 1	Lift up your heads, O gates!
Reader 2	and be lifted up, O ancient doors!
Reader 3	that the King of Glory may come in.

"Praise the Lord!" (Psalm 150)

Reader 4	Who is the King of glory?
Reader 5	The Lord, strong and mighty.
Reader 6	The Lord, mighty in battle!
Reader 7	Lift up your heads, O gates!
Reader 8	and be lifted up, O ancient doors!
Reader 9	that the King of glory may come in.
Reader 10	Who is this King of glory?
Reader 11	The Lord of Hosts,
Reader 12	he is the King of glory!

Solo and Chorus

Often in Hebrew poetry an idea is stated on one line and the same idea is stated again in the following line in a little different way. Notice how this is true in this psalm.

Psalm 95:1-7 (RSV)

Solo	O come, let us sing to the Lord,
Class	let us make a joyful noise to the rock of our salvation!

Solo	Let us come into his presence with thanksgiving;
Class	let us make a joyful noise to him with songs of praise!
Solo	For the LORD is a great God,
Class	and a great King above all gods.
Solo	In his hands are the depths of the earth;
Class	the heights of the mountains are his also.
Solo	The sea is his, for he made it;
Class	for his hands formed the dry land.
Solo	O come, let us worship and bow down,
Class	let us kneel before the LORD, our Maker!
Solo	For he is our God,
Class	and we are the people of his pasture and the sheep of his hand.

Unison Reading

The entire class reads together.

Psalm 133 (RSV)

Behold, how good and pleasant it is
  when brothers dwell in unity!
It is like the precious oil upon the head,
  running down upon the beard,
upon the beard of Aaron,
  running down on the collar of his robes!
It is like the dew of Hermon,
  which falls on the mountains of Zion!
For there the LORD has commanded the blessing,
  life for evermore.

The class may wish to take the theme of "brothers" (people) dwelling in unity and describe or rewrite its delight in more contemporary terms. How do we see people dwelling in unity in our society? What, in our society, is like the "dew of Hermon" or the "oil upon the head"?

Additional Activities:

1. Find in the psalms examples of:
   —praise to God
   —repentance

—thanksgiving
—petition

2. The psalms are special to us not only because of their beauty, but because they express our longings and prayers to God. Find in the psalms a sentence that expresses feelings you have had.

3. Many psalms create visual images in our minds. The class might wish to illustrate scenes from these four psalms:
—Psalm 107:23, 24
—Psalm 121:1
—Psalm 23:2
—Psalm 100:4

NINTH WAY . . . READERS' THEATER

Readers' Theater is another way to use the written word as a vehicle for drama. This method eliminates the need for memorizing. It focuses on the factual rather than the spontaneous.

Students sit in front of a class and read, in a dramatic way, a play or dramatic episode. The important thing is the reading, so it is necessary to use persons with some experience in drama or a feel for dramatic reading. Many portions of the Bible can be read like Readers' Theater. The first chapter of the book of Job is read by four students sitting on high stools in front of the class.

This reading can serve as an introduction to the study of the book of Job, or it can stand alone as a devotional reading.

Job

(BASED ON JOB: 1)

Student 1—the narrator
Student 2—Satan, Servant 2, and Servant 4
Student 3—Servant 1 and Servant 3
Student 4—God and Job

The Reading

Student 1

There was a man named Job who worshiped God and lived in the land of Uz. Job was faithful to God. He was a good man, careful not to do anything evil. He had seven sons and three daughters and owned seven thousand sheep, three thousand camels, one thousand head of cattle, and five hundred donkeys. He also had a large number of servants and was the richest man in the East. Job's sons used to take turns giving a feast to which all the others would come, and they always invited their three sisters. The morning after each feast, Job would get up early and offer sacrifices for each of his children in order to purify them. He always did this because he thought that one of them might have sinned by insulting God unintentionally. When the day came for the heavenly beings to appear before the Lord, Satan was there among them.

Student 4 (God)

What have you been doing?

Student 2 (Satan)

I have been walking here and there, roaming around the earth.

Student 4

Did you notice my servant Job? There is no one on earth as faithful and good as he is. He worships me and is careful not to do anything evil.

Student 2	Would Job worship you if he got nothing out of it? You have always protected him and his family and everything he owns. You bless everything he does and you have given him enough cattle to fill the whole country. But now suppose you take away everything he has—he will curse you to your face!
Student 4	All right, everything he has is in your power, but you must not hurt Job.
Student 1	One day a messenger came running to Job.
Student 3	We were plowing the fields with the oxen, and the donkeys were in a nearby pasture. Suddenly the Sabeans attacked and stole them all. They killed every one of your servants except me. I am the only one who escaped to tell you.
Student 1	Before he had finished speaking, another servant came and said:
Student 2	Lightning struck the sheep and the shepherds and killed them all. I am the only one who escaped to tell you.
Student 1	Before he had finished speaking another servant came and said:
Student 2	Three bands of Chaldean raiders attacked us, took away the camels and killed all your servants except me. I am the only one who escaped to tell you.
Student 1	Before he had finished speaking another servant came and said:
Student 2	Your children were having a feast at the home of your oldest son when a storm swept in from the desert. It blew the house down and killed them all. I am the only one who escaped to tell you.
Student 1	Then Job got up and tore his clothes in grief. He shaved his head and threw himself face downward on the ground.
Student 4	I was born with nothing and I will die with nothing. The Lord gave, and now God has taken away. May God's name be praised!
Student 1	In spite of everything that had happened, Job did not sin by blaming God.

"The LORD gave, and now he has taken away." (Job 1:21)

USING WORDS AND ACTION TOGETHER

CHAPTER FOUR

TENTH WAY . . . ROLE-PLAY

We have looked at body movement, sounds, and words. Now we will put them together in role-play. Role-playing is the spontaneous acting out of a problem situation in human relationships, followed by a discussion of what happened in the situation and why. This method of drama can be a form of therapy, with the purpose of changing the attitudes or the behavior of the individual or group. However, trained leadership is recommended for such therapy, so leave this to the professional psychologist. For our purposes, role-play will be used to help teach the Bible by letting the students put themselves into a biblical situation and experience how a person in that situation might feel and act.

In studying the Bible, a tantalizing question is: What happened next? Fragments of situations and characters and actions flash for a moment on the Bible scene and then we hear no more. These are ready-made situations for role-playing. Let's look, for example, at the story of the boy with the five loaves and two fishes. How would we develop this story for role-playing?

Boy with Loaves and Fishes
(BASED ON JOHN 6:1-13)

Instructions:

—Read together John 6:1-13
—Ask the students to share their ideas of what they think happened next. We hear no more about this boy in the Bible. What would he have done immediately after this?
—Have each person decide which of the following roles to take: the boy, his mother, his friend, his brother.
—Help the students develop their own interpretations of the roles they have taken. The teacher never offers suggestions for playing the roles, but does help the student clarify the role by asking questions, such as:

To the Boy—Why did you go to the hillside to hear Jesus? Had you heard him before? What did you think of him? How did you feel when he took your loaves and fishes?

To the Mother—Had you packed the lunch for the boy? Did you know where he was going that day? What have you heard about this man Jesus? How do you feel about your son now?

They all ate and had enough. (Luke 9:17)

To the Friend—How well do you know the boy? Why were you together that day? Did you want to go and hear Jesus? How do you feel about what happened on the hillside?

To the Brother—How do you feel about your brother? Why did you not go to the hillside that day? Why don't you believe the story they are telling? Are you younger or older than your brother? Why do you think he is telling this story?

—Briefly review the situation: The miracle of Jesus feeding the multitude with a boy's lunch of five loaves and two fishes has just occurred. The boy is rushing home with his friend to tell the family about what happened.

—When the students playing the roles are ready, the situation is spontaneously enacted. The rest of the class watches the action. The teacher may wish to assign certain members of the class to observe a specific character.

—Cut the action after two or three minutes. This may occur when a climax seems to have been reached or when the characters seem to be running out of dialogue. Don't let the role-play go so long that interest lags or the people involved cannot think of anything more to say.

—Discuss the role-play. What happened, and why?

This is the time when members of the group try to understand how the persons in the situation felt and why they acted as they did. The teacher must guide the discussion so that judgment will not be given on the *acting skill* of the players. Remember, the purpose of role-playing is not to present a dramatic production. The purpose is to observe and experience a situation first-hand.

Depending on the size of the class and interest in the story, the teacher may want to provide the opportunity for other students to take on the roles and do another role-play.

Role-playing is suggested for fifth grade through high school. An interesting role-play for the teenage years might be: What happened next to the rich young ruler? (Luke 18).

Role-playing can be used again and again in your church school class. An entire book of the Bible, such as Ruth, can be studied in this way over a period of weeks. Be sure to have resource books on hand—Bible commentaries, Bible dictionaries, books on people of the Bible, a geography of the Bible, and books on life in Bible times—for the students to use as they seek to developthe characters.

CHAPTER FIVE

*I*n drama, we try to see life through another person's eyes. We try to become that person and experience as much as possible what that person might have felt. Some people find it easier to do this "under cover." Rather that be on an open stage or in front of a class, it is easier for some to act behind puppets or masks, or even in shadows. In that way, there is a freedom to play a role without inhibitions. Without being on display, a child may find it easier to "let go."

ELEVENTH WAY . . . PUPPETS

What is more fun than puppets? They are fun to create, fun to act behind, and fun to watch. They open a whole world of drama. Puppets can be as simple as a piece of cloth with a face painted on it and wrapped around your hand, or as elaborate as a paper-mache head with a complete wardrobe of changeable costumes. With imagination a puppet can appear from a paper sack, a raw potato, an old rubber ball, a sock, a box, or a wooden spoon.

There are myriad ways to use puppets in religious education. The following is one suggestion of a way to make a biblical teaching take on meaning for a child.

The Pharisee and the Tax Collector
(BASED ON LUKE 18:9-14)

The purpose of this activity is to give children first-hand experience in creating puppets and to teach the parable of the Pharisee and the tax collector. Before beginning to make the puppets, read Luke 18:9-14 with the class. Tell the students ahead of time that they will be making puppets to act out this story. Ask them to try to picture in their minds what each of the characters might look like as they read the story. After reading the Scripture passage, read the play to the class. Hearing the play will help the students develop the characters.

The two puppets suggested for this play use a simple basic design, shaped to fit a child's hand. Cut two pieces of cloth. Sew together as shown in the illustration. Turn inside out. Draw a face on the puppet head. The thumb forms one of the puppet's hands, the second and third fingers form the head, and the fourth finger forms the other hand.

One puppet could be elaborately dressed in rich colors, with perhaps a prayer shawl and a fancy hat made from a paper nut cup. The face looks haughty. Perhaps it should have a beard. The other puppet should be more simple, with a humble face, and using basic colors. But these are only suggestions.

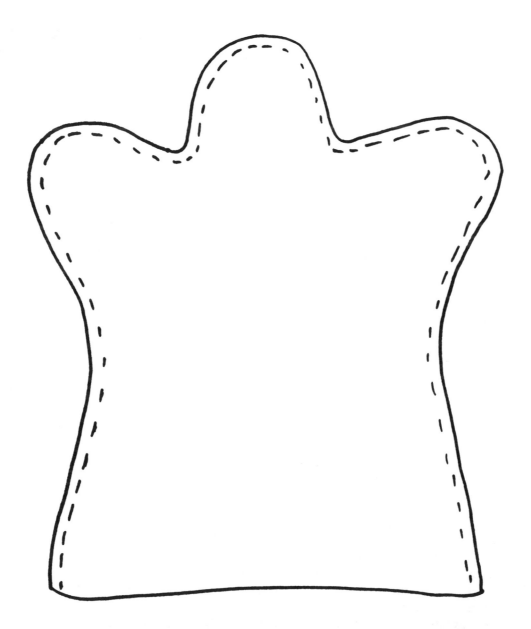

The fun of creating puppets is to do your own thing. Have a variety of materials on hand—scissors, glue, yarn, felt , magic markers, needle and thread. Let the children choose their materials and create the image they have of the characters.

After the puppets are constructed, let the children work with them, get acquainted, improvise conversations, talk to them and through them.

Getting Ready:

Props — The only prop in this play is a coin. This should be oversized for easy handling and so it can be easily seen by the audience.

Cast — Two children for puppet actors—a Pharisee and a Tax Collector. They will speak only once. The rest of their parts will be action.
— One or two children for the Reader's part.
— Two children to hold a rug or bedspread taut to form a stage.
— A puppet for everyone. Though this play uses only two, let each child have the experience of creating a puppet; repeat the play a number of times.

The Puppet Show

(Pharisee puppet pops up from center stage)

Pharisee: Hello. I'm a Pharisee.
(waves to audience)

Reader: In the days of Jesus, the Pharisees were a group of Jews dedicated to keeping the Jewish law in exact detail. There were six hundred commandments, which it was their duty to keep and to see that other people did so too. Is that right, Pharisee?
(puppet nods head)

Reader: The Pharisees thought that obedience to every little bit of Jewish law was necessary in order to be God's servant. When Jesus said there was a new and better way, did the Pharisees understand?
(puppet shakes head)

Reader: Well, thank you. We'll find out more about this in our play.
(Pharisee puppet leaves; Tax Collector puppet pops up)

Tax Collector: Hello. I'm a tax collector.
(bows to audience)

Reader: In Jesus' day a tax collector was the person who collected taxes from the people for the Romans.
(Tax Collector picks up a large piece of money, shows audience; drops coin behind curtain)

Reader: The people did not like the tax collectors because they often tried to take more money than they were supposed to.
(Tax Collector bows head in shame)

Reader: The tax collectors also were hated because they mixed with Gentiles and even had meals with them.
(Tax Collector bows head all the way to the floor)

Reader: Now, don't feel bad. You are the hero of this story.
              (Tax Collector perks up and pops below stage)

Reader: O.K. Are we ready to begin?
              (Second Reader may take over here)

Reader: Two men went up to the Temple to pray. One was a Pharisee,
              (Pharisee glides on stage very slowly and grandly like a king)

Reader: and the other was a tax collector.
              (Tax Collector creeps slowly on stage)

Reader: The Pharisee stood apart by himself
              (Pharisee looks at the Tax Collector and turns his back on him)

Reader: and prayed: "God, I thank you that I am not like other men—
              (throws both hands to sky)

Reader: greedy, dishonest, immoral.
              (sways back and forth)

Reader: I fast two days a week.
              (points proudly to himself)

Reader: I give one-tenth of all my income."
              (hands on hips proudly, head back to sky)

Reader: But the tax collector stood at a distance and beat upon his breast
              (Tax Collector beats breast)

Reader: and said, "O God, have mercy on me, a sinner."
              (Tax Collector bows head to floor)

Reader: Jesus said, "I tell you, the tax collector, not the Pharisee, was in the right with God when he went home. For everyone who makes himself great will be humbled, and everyone who humbles himself will be made great."
              (Tax Collector claps hands in joy; Pharisee creeps off stage)

Follow Up:

After the play, invite responses from the class. Some questions you might ask to facilitate discussion:

What new facts did you learn about tax collectors and Pharisees?
How did some of you show the characters of the Pharisee and the tax collector in the construction of your puppets?
How did you see the characteristics of the two people in the actions of the puppets?
Who are some people you can think of in our society who are like the Pharisee and the tax collector?
Why do you think Jesus told this parable?

Use the puppets to act out other parables from the Bible and to create your own parables. If your class catches the very contagious puppet fever, you will want to learn more in this field. There are a host of books and films and pamphlets available to give you ideas. Especially helpful is the chapter on making puppets in *Creative Activities in Church Education,* by Patricia Griggs.

TWELFTH WAY . . . MASKS

Along the Via Dolorosa

Masks have been known for thousands of years. Far back in history, masks were used to help people become better actors. Just as with puppets, there are many ways to create and use masks. Simple masks can be made from paper plates, pillowcases, paper bags, or leftover Halloween masks. More elaborate masks can be constructed from paper-mache, Latex, Claycrete or Celastic. Makeup, with paint and putty placed directly on the face, is also a kind of mask. Students can wear masks while playing any biblical character, in pantomime or with dialogue.

One of the advantages of masks is that they are an excellent means of expressing emotions. Their exaggerated expressions can help the actor and the audience understand exactly how a character feels.

A play using masks is called a masque. In the following masque, students are asked to go back emotionally and mentally two thousand years, to the first Good Friday—the time of Jesus' crucifixion. As Jesus dragged his cross along the Via Dolorosa in Jerusalem, a crowd gathered to watch. In that crowd were people with all the human emotions—hate, love, worry, surprise, sadness, anger, fear. Students will be given a number of identities—characters who might have been present in Jerusalem—and each student will then create a mask depicting his or her character's feelings.

Directions for Masks:

Each person will need a grocery bag (No. 20 for children, larger for adults), scissors, and felt-tip pens or crayons.

Cut a fringe all the way around the bottom of the bag so it will rest well down on the student's shoulders without twisting or teetering.

Slip the bag over the head. Carefully mark the eyes and nose. Take off the bag and cut out holes at the spots you have marked. When the holes are cut in the right places, the students are ready to decorate their masks. If they wish, they may glue things to the masks, but the emotions will probably be better conveyed if only a pen or crayon is used.

Identities:

Money Changer. These men set up their stands in the court of the Temple. If worshipers wished to give money, it had to be in the local coinage minted at Tyre. So there was a lot of changing of money and much trickery in doing so. On Monday Jesus had driven the money changers out of the Temple (read Matt. 21:12,13).

Peter, who had just denied three times that he knew Jesus. But Peter was very close to Jesus and had boldly said that Jesus was the Christ, the Son of God. Jesus had given him the name "Peter," which means *rock.*

Pharisee. The Pharisees were a group of Jews dedicated to keeping the Jewish law in every exact detail. Jesus was angry with them because they could not see beyond the little points of the law to the larger law of love, and he often said things that discounted their way of life.

Child who had waved branches the week before (on Palm Sunday). Use your imagination.

Lazarus of Bethany. Jesus often visited in the home of Lazarus and his two sisters, Mary and Martha. On Wednesday, just before the betrayal and trial, Jesus had been at their home.

Salome, the mother of James and John, disciples of Jesus. Use your imagination.

Lawyer. Lawyers in the time of Jesus were men skilled in the observances of the Jewish law. They had been watching Jesus and trying to trick him. Jesus believed it was better to be loving and helpful than to keep the exact letter of the law.

Stranger, who had never heard of Jesus. Use your imagination.

Roman Soldier. Roman soldiers were usually citizens of Rome who volunteered for service in the army. In peace time their job was to keep order in the streets and guard prisoners who were being taken about. It was their business to see to the details of execution.

Slave. Slavery was taken for granted in the first century. Although it was usual to allow slaves holidays at public festivals, they were the property of their master who could do with them as he wished. Jesus taught about the worth of every individual soul and that all are equal in God's sight.

Woman Healed by Jesus. One day she saw Jesus and, not wanting to disturb him but wanting to be cured of an illness she had had for many years, came up behind him and touched his coat, believing she would be made well. And she was.

Boy who had been on the hillside and given the disciples his lunch to help feed the crowd that had come to listen to Jesus.

Instructions:

—Have each class member choose an identity. (You and the students might want to add more identities to choose from.)
—Allow time for the students to think about their characters. How would the person be feeling? What emotion would be showing on the person's face?
—Construct the masks.
—Give everyone time to decide on a few lines to say that will express the character's feelings and further convey the expression on the mask.
—Everyone puts on the masks and takes a position in the crowd.
—Imagine Jesus approaching, dragging his cross.
—Spontaneously react, with students expressing the feelings they have decided on.
—Afterward, let each person tell the class the emotion he or she was trying to express. Would any disagree with the emotions expressed? Were they believable? Would people really feel like that? Do we have the same emotions? Do the students have suggestions to offer one another on the portrayal of their characters?
—After the discussion, do a revised version of the masque, incorporating the suggestions.

THIRTEENTH WAY . . . SHADOW PLAYS

There is a kind of magic in shadows. Who among us has not made shadow figures as a child, jumping about to form a giant, a circus skinny-man, a tiny dwarf; or created wonderful animals on the wall with the magic of hands and shadows. This is a form of drama (acting under cover) and an intriguing method to bring into our church school classrooms. Perhaps the most fun of all is a shadow play, a dramatic story acted out with shadows. The players act in pantomime while a narrator and the voice parts stand off-screen and tell the story portrayed in the shadows. A sheet or screen may be attached across the front of a stage, between two pillars in a room, or a classroom door. The actors stand behind the sheet with a bright light behind them, which makes their shadows on the sheet. Since shadow plays are excellent ways to dramatize stories in which there are great differences in the size of things to be represented, the story of David and Goliath is a natural. One's shadow becomes smaller as one moves toward the screen and away from the light, and larger as one moves away from the screen and closer to the light. So it is possible for children to create images of both a life-size David and an oversized Goliath. Though this story may be less to the liking of the teacher, ten- and eleven-year-olds, especially, will like the physical bravery of David. This story will be most helpful if David's faith that God will help him is stressed as the main point of the story.

The purpose of this activity is to acquaint children with the method of shadow drama through the story of David and Goliath, and to learn the story through enacting it.

David and Goliath
(BASED ON I SAMUEL 17)

Instructions:

A good shadow play grows from itself. It develops by trying things one way and then another, looking carefully at effects and finding the way that is best. There will need to be a lot of experimenting in front of the light. You may want to use a group of children as "directors" to plan the scenes. There are four shadow scenes:

Scene 1: Goliath Challenges the Israelites
Scene 2: David Before King Saul
Scene 3: David and Goliath Meet in Battle
Scene 4: David Again Before the King

The cast includes: Shadow Figures—Goliath, David, Saul
Voices—Goliath, David, Saul, Narrator

Perhaps the greatest difference between a shadow play and a regular play is in the costumes and props. Imagination is the main requirement of shadow costuming. All that matters is the result—how it looks in shadow. A pan on Goliath's head may make the shadow of a perfect helmet. Props are flat—probably best made from cardboard. Goliath's sword and David's staff and basket may be made this way. Headdress is important, and you will want to give attention to Saul's crown and Goliath's helmet.

The actors act in profile. Facial expression won't show, and body movements should be exaggerated and probably more slow than usual.

The Play

Narrator: The nation of Israel was in trouble. An enemy, the Philistine nation, had gathered an army to fight King Saul and the men of Israel. Farmers and herdsmen from Israel left their homes and went forth to fight. The two armies marched out and stood facing each other across a plain. Now the Philistines had a mighty warrior, a giant named Goliath. Every morning Goliath strode out and challenged Israel.
(light on screen; shadow figure of Goliath appears; he stands legs akimbo, shaking fist)

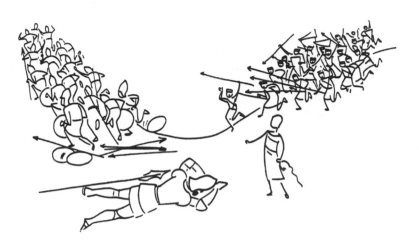

David defeated and killed Goliath. (I Sam. 17:51)

But none dared face him because he was so strong and so well armed, with his helmet of bronze, his coat of mail, his thick spear and mighty sword.

Voice of Goliath: I defy the armies of Israel this day. Give me a man, that we can fight together.
(David appears on one side of screen, close up, carrying basket)

Narrator: Now David, a shepherd boy, came to the camp of the Israelites, bearing food for his brothers who were soldiers. He heard Goliath's morning challenge and was horrified to see all the Israelite soldiers shrink back in fear.

Voice of David: Who is this Philistine who defies the army of the living God?
(light out)

Narrator: But David's brothers were angry with him and told him to go back to minding sheep and leave war to the men. Instead, David went to the tent of King Saul.
(light on; king is seated in profile, crown on his head; David enters and kneels before him)

Voice of David: I will go out and fight this Philistine.

Narrator: But the king saw only a boy before him.

Voice of Saul: You are only a lad. Goliath has been a soldier all his life.

Voice of David: I am a shepherd. Both a lion and a bear have taken lambs from my flock. Both I hunted, and both I killed. The Lord went with me and protected me from the talon of the lion and the claw of the bear. He will shield me from this Philistine.

Narrator: Then the king answered, speaking slowly and solemnly.

Voice of Saul:	So be it. And the Lord go with you. *(light out)*
Narrator:	David was outfitted in a coat of gleaming armor. He was given the army's mightiest sword and a helmet of brass. But when little David was clothed in all the heavy armor, he could not walk.
Voice of David:	No! I shall get nowhere in these.
Narrator:	He took off the heavy armor, gathered five smooth stones from the stream and put them his shepherd's pouch. Then, with his good oak staff in one hand and his shepherd's sling in the other, he walked out to meet Goliath. *(light on; Goliath stands close to light in all his armor; David stands close to screen)*
Narrator:	When Goliath saw David, he threw back his head and laughed. How he laughed! *(Goliath pantomimes action)*
Voice of Goliath:	Am I a dog that you come with a stick? Come to me. *(beckons David with his finger)* Come, little one, and I will feed your flesh to the crows. *(swings mighty sword)*
Narrator:	David stood just outside the range of Goliath's spear and called in a clear voice that rang across the plains.
Voice of David:	Goliath, you come with sword and spear and shield. But I come armed with the name of the Lord, the God of Israel. Today God will deliver you into my hands. Goliath, I am going to kill you, and both these armies will know that the salvation of the Lord God is not to be won with sword and spear. *(David fits stone into his sling and in slow motion hurls it at the giant)*
Narrator:	Straight the stone flew, like an arrow to a target. It hit the giant in the forehead, just below his helmet. *(Goliath collapses slowly—first onto his knees, clutching his forehead, then onto the ground; light out)*
Narrator:	A great cheer went up from the army of Israel. And when the Philistines saw that their champion was dead, they ran away. So the day ended with a great victory for Israel! *(light on; King Saul on throne; David comes and kneels before him)*
Narrator:	David came again to King Saul and knelt before him. He asked if he might enter Saul's service. He swore allegiance to King Saul and became his armor bearer. Later this brave boy, who put his trust in God rather than in weapons, became the new king of Israel.

Though the main purpose of this play is to introduce children to shadow drama, this play could be used to initiate a study of David. Students could research the life of David for other ways in which he expressed his faith that God would uphold him.

This could be used in another way as a teaching method. The teacher could read the narrator and voice parts to the class, encouraging the students to form pictures in their minds of the action. With the screen and light in place, call on members of the class to create the shadow picture they see, using fellow students to help them. The students would stand just where and in whatever pose the "director" places them.

ACTING USING ELECTRONIC EQUIPMENT

CHAPTER SIX

Our modern technology has given us other ways of acting under cover. These give us the same benefits as puppets or masks, with the added benefit of appealing to the mechanically minded child. Tape recorders are a common resource, as are slide projectors and movie equipment. Some church schools are fortunate enough to have closed-circuit TV, and many have video equipment.

FOURTEENTH WAY . . . TAPE-RECORDER PLAYS

Tape-recorder plays are a good choice for church school drama. There are no memorized lines, and each person in the class can take part. Most students like to hear the sound of their own voices. Sound effects are an important part of tape-recorder plays because the whole story must be told in words and sounds, since there is no way to see what people in the story are doing. You can use the recorder spontaneously. For example, you could record your role-playing dramas. Or you could make the tape recorder drama an end in itself, as in the following drama.

Creation

(BASED ON GENESIS 1–2)

The purpose of using a tape recorder to teach the Creation story is to evoke reverence and wonder through sounds and reading. This is a story of immense mystery and beauty. Besides learning the story, students should learn something of the great awe in this story.

Instructions:

This project is suggested for teenagers. It utilizes some musical ability. An electric instrument (organ, electric piano, or guitar) is needed as well as these instruments: xylophone, drum (with heavy stick and wire brushes), tambourine, cymbals, small bells. Other sound-effects are to be made vocally or with simple everyday supplies. Using a tape recorder, it is possible to record one sound, then turn off the tape while you prepare the properties necessary for the next sound. Don't feel bound by the script, but allow the class to be creative in the development of sounds.

The Recording

Reader: In the beginning, the earth was without form, and darkness was upon the face of the deep.

(electronic sounds to create the feeling of the lack of form in the unfinished world—electric

piano, organ, or guitar in unrelated, dissonant sounds; wild and unformed; sound continues with voice over it)

Reader: But the spirit of God was moving over the face of the water.
(percussion sounds, perhaps drum beat, begins to sound through the dissonance; order is beginning to develop from the original chaos; sounds begin to become more formed, leading to silence and the next spoken word)

Reader: And God said:

Dark Voice: *(use megaphone to amplify)* Let there be light!
(open, spreading sound, like several octave glissandos on piano or xylophone)

Reader: Water covered the earth.
(sea sounds—use wire brushes on a drum; experiment until you get the effect you want)

Reader: And God separated the waters from the waters and made a firmament.
(splashing water sounds—dip hands in and out of a bucket of water to create effect)

Reader: And God said:

Dark Voice: Let the waters under the heavens be gathered together in one place, and let the dry land appear.
(wind sound—make a sort of whistling sound without really whistling: pucker the lips and let the air escape through the mouth with less speed and force than it would take to whistle; three people perform in rotation, overlapping one another)

Reader: And it was so. God called the dry land earth and the waters that were gathered together he called seas. And God said:

Dark Voice: Let the earth put forth vegetation—plants yielding seed, and fruit trees bearing fruit in which is their seed, each according to its kind upon the earth.
(rustling sound—shake a tambourine or put a cupful of uncooked rice in the bottom of a small box and shake gently)

Reader: The earth brought forth vegetation. And God said:

Dark Voice: Let there be lights in the firmament of the heavens to separate the day from the night.
(cymbal or gong hit with a stick; overtones should give mysterious sound)

Reader: And there was the sun and the moon and the stars.
(sparkling, tinkling sound of small bells)

Reader: And God said:

Dark Voice: Let the waters bring forth swarms of living creatures, and let birds fly above the earth across the firmament of the heavens.
(use water sounds; for birds' flapping wings, hold a folded newspaper in one hand and slap the corner of it rapidly with the finger of the other)

Reader: Then God said:

Dark Voice: Let the earth bring forth living creatures: cattle and creeping things and beasts of the earth, each according to its kind.
(cattle sound—"moo" into a bucket or cupped hands; intensify imitated roar of lion or tiger by making the noise through a funnel shape)

Reader: And then God thought, there must be something to have dominion over the fish of the sea and over the birds of the air and over the cattle and over all the earth and every creeping thing upon the earth. And so God said:

Dark Voice: Let us make humans in our image, after our own likeness.
(loud clash of cymbals)

Reader: God created people in the image of God, male and female were created. God blessed them. Here was not merely the most complicated or the most beautiful animal, but a spiritual being able to know God and to respond to God.
(may end with a sound of great glory or with a glorious hymn)

Follow up:

The students may want to make slides to go along with their tape. They also may wish to do a serious study, comparing the Creation stories found in Genesis (see Griggs, *Twenty Ways of Teaching the Bible*, pp. 18-19, "Comparing the Creation Stories").

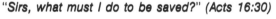
"Sirs, what must I do to be saved?" (Acts 16:30)

Paul in Prison at Philippi
(BASED ON ACTS 16:16-40)

Here is a less symbolic tape-recorder play for use in a classroom setting. It may be used in the same unit of study as "On the Road to Damascus," and with the same age-level children.

The purpose of this drama is to give children the experience of creating a tape-recorder play so that the story of Paul in prison at Philippi may take on more meaning.

Instructions:

—This play encourages the students to make sounds and use their voices to create a Bible story. Do not feel it is necessary to use the exact sounds suggested, but encourage your class to create its own. For example, you might ask: How do you think an earthquake would sound? What are some ways we can create sounds of chains falling? Experiment with some sounds—wind, earthquake, shouts of joy. Have two volunteers read the solo parts, and select others to be responsible for the following sounds:

    door slamming
    the wind (whooooo)
    earthquake (tambourines shaking or whatever sound you wish to create)
    chains (rattle bracelets)
    sing hymn together (choose joyful hymn that the whole class knows)
    shouts of joy (Yeah!)

—Set the stage for the drama by reading the following:

Paul was imprisoned many times for his faith. He was arrested in Philippi and Jerusalem, imprisoned for two years at Caesarea and held prisoner for at least two years in Rome. While he was imprisoned at Philippi, a strange thing happened. We want to make this story come alive by creating sound effects and taping them with the story.

The Play

Reader: Paul and Silas had been arrested earlier in the day, then beaten and thrown into prison without trial. They were placed in the inner cell with thick, damp, stone walls, and chains were locked around their feet.
        (rattling sound of chains)

It was about midnight, and Paul and Silas and the other prisoners were singing hymns.
        (class sings hymn)

Suddenly they heard the wind beginning to blow—first softly, then wilder and wilder.
        (sound of wind)

Paul felt a slight tremor.
        (tambourine starts)

Then the thick stone walls began to quiver.
        (tambourine louder and faster)

Soon the whole prison was shaking in an earthquake.
        (tambourine still louder and faster, plus wind sounds)

Immediately the doors to the prison, which had been bolted and latched, banged open.
        (doors slam)

And all the prisoners' chains fell off.
(jangling of bracelets)

A great shout went up from the prisoners.
(Yeah!)

The jailer, who was responsible for the prisoners, awoke and saw the doors open. He knew it would bring great disgrace upon him if the prisoners escaped. In utter despair he drew his sword and was about to kill himself, when Paul called out with a loud voice:

Solo 1:   Do not harm yourself, for we are all here.

Reader: The jailer called for light.

Solo 2:   Quick, bring the torches.

Reader: And trembling, he fell before Paul and Silas and said:

Solo 2:   What must I do to be saved?

Reader: And they told him to believe in the Lord Jesus.

Some Sample Follow-up Questions:

1. Why do you think Paul did not escape? (Read Acts 16:32-40 to discover what happened next.)
2. Paul wrote letters from his prisons. What does the class think Paul would have written about while in prison? What would members of the class write about if they were in prison? To whom would they write? Compare their answers with what Paul did.
3. Read Romans 8:28. What do you think Paul meant? What good did Paul think would come from his experience in prison? What good came from his experience at Philippi?
4. Brainstorm all the feelings you think the jailer was experiencing.

FIFTEENTH WAY . . . SLIDE SHOWS

Students from fifth grade up are able to create and produce 16mm movies or 35mm slide shows. Such a project can be fun for all concerned, but more important, it can deepen your students' appreciation and understanding of certain portions of the Bible.

The Beatitudes (Matt. 5:1-12) are such a familiar part of our Scriptures that sometimes their reading falls on ears that are not really listening. To use the Beatitudes as the basis for a slide show would help your students study more deeply their meaning for our lives today. The following project is suggested:

Use a 35mm camera and color film. For indoor photography you will need a flash attachment. For outdoors a light meter will be helpful, unless you have a camera that has automatic features. Using different settings, take several shots of each scene to be sure you get a good one.

Instructions:

After you have asked the students to listen closely to the words of Jesus and to try to apply those words to our present-day lives, read the Beatitudes together. Then allow a few minutes for the students to share the way they think Jesus' words apply to our lives today. Then work through the meaning of each Beatitude and decide how it could be illustrated with a slide. To help in this process, ask questions such as these:

1. *Spiritually Poor.* What do you think it means to be poor in Spirit? What types of people in our society do you think would fall in this category? Why? How would you express this in a slide?
2. *Those Who Mourn.* What are some examples of mourning that you have seen or experienced? (Brainstorm as many ideas as you can think of, then decide which of these could be illustrated by a slide.)
3. *Those Who Are Humble.* What does the word *humble* mean? (Look it up in the dictionary.) What kinds of people would you consider humble? How could these people and this idea be conveyed in a slide?
4. *Those Whose Greatest Desire Is to Do What God Requires.* What are some things you think God requires? What are some examples of actions that show we are doing what God requires? How can we show this in a slide?
5. *The Merciful.* What are some contemporary examples of mercy? (Look at the newspaper or a current magazine.) How can we show this in a slide?
6. *The Pure in Heart.* Who is the most pure person you know? Is it a child? An older person? What makes that person "pure in heart"? How can we capture this quality in a slide?
7. *Those Who Work for Peace.* What image comes to your mind when you hear "work for peace"? Do you think of diplomats settling wars, or children settling quarrels, or actions of people who are loving and kind? How do you want to express this in a slide?
8. *Those Who Are Persecuted Because They Do What God Requires.* In what ways are persons persecuted? (You may want to look up the word *persecuted*.) Who are some people being persecuted today for doing what God requires? How can we show this in a slide?
9. *People Who Are Insulted and Lied About Because They Are Followers of Jesus.* Why do you think someone who follows Jesus might be the subject of such treatment? What are some things followers of Jesus might do that would cause people to insult them and tell lies about them? How can we show this in a slide?

Decide on the details of each picture.
   — Who will be in the picture?
   — What will they be doing?
   — What properties will you need?
   — Will you need any costumes?
   — What is a good background for the scene? (Where should the picture be taken?)
   — Do you need the help of someone outside the class?

Assemble the things you need, then create the scenes and take the photographs. After the slides have been developed, have the students select the ones they wish to use and rewrite the final script to tell the story. Show the slides while one or more students read the script. You may decide to share the slide show with another class. The slides could become a permanent part of your audiovisual resources.

SIXTEENTH WAY . . . VIDEO DRAMA

Your own video can be made as elaborate as a modern-day movie or as simple as a film of your friends. Churches are finding numerous ways to use this equipment—from a spontaneous filming of a church school classroom, to interviews, to full-fledged dramatic productions. The following play is suggested as a video for fifth- and sixth-graders. It uses two settings, exterior and interior.

Jesus Answers His Enemies' Question

(BASED ON JOHN 8:1-11)

Equipment Needed:

—*A Video Cassette Recorder (VCR)*. Most VCRs are small and portable. A VCR operates along the same general lines as an audio-tape recorder, except that it records the picture along with the sound on a compact, self-contained video cassette. Most contain an audio-dub which makes it possible to add narration and music to the sound track.

—*A Portable Video Camera*. A standard camera offers a fixed lens and an optional viewfinder and built-in microphone. A deluxe camera will have zoom lens for close-ups and an electronic viewfinder, plus other extras.

—*A Cart* for the video recorder is necessary unless your VCR has a shoulder strap, because the recorder must accompany the camera while the recording is being done.

—*A TV Set* on which to show the finished film.

Persons Needed:

—One or two students to work the camera.

—A teacher or student to be the director.

—Nine actors (Though the enemies of Jesus are described as men, they may be played by boys or girls.)

—One or more students to decide on the set and get it ready. These students will choose the location for filming and collect all the props.

Rehearse the play several times before filming it, to save time and achieve a better finished product.

The Play

Shot One—Title

(*Hold the camera on the title approximately twice as long as it takes to read it. This will allow even the slowest readers to finish reading before the next shot comes on the screen. The title may be handwritten or you might use a titling kit from a photo store.*)

Shot Two—Credits

(*Names of the cast, director, camera operator, set designers, etc.*)

SCENE 1

Shot Three—Long shot; narrator sitting in chair.

Narrator: Good evening, ladies and gentlemen.
        (*turns to camera*)

Shot Four—Close-up of narrator.

Narrator: We are bringing you an episode from the life of Jesus. Summer has passed and the cooler days of autumn have arrived. It is the time of the Feast of Tabernacles in Jerusalem. Visitors from every part of the world have crowded into the city. They are talking about the great teacher of Galilee whose miracles have caused much excitement in many places. Jesus has appeared in the Temple to teach the people.

Shot Five—Cut to another angle.

Narrator: *(turns to camera)* The enemies of Jesus are looking for a chance to capture him. The chief priests of the Temple, the scribes, and the Pharisees and Sadducees are jealous of Jesus because he drew the attention of the people who came to the feast. They dislike his teaching because he accused them of only pretending to be righteous. They are watching for some fault, some false word. For days, Jesus has sat in the temple, teaching all who came to him, and no one could find fault. But the enemies of Jesus have hit upon a plan. They will go themselves and ask him a question concerning the teaching of the Law of Moses.

SCENE II

Shot Six—Exterior; long shot to establish setting.
(Jesus standing on sand-covered ground; stones of various sizes are around him.)

Shot Seven—Long shot—continuous action in one unbroken take.
(several men, holding a woman, walk straight to Jesus; camera follows action)

Shot Eight—Medium shot of group.

First Man: Master, this woman is very wicked, and in the Law, Moses has commanded that such a person should be stoned until she dies.

Second Man: But what do you say we shall do with her?

Other Men: *(ad lib)* Yeah? What do you think? You're a great teacher, what's your advice? Come on. Tell us. etc.

Shot Nine—Close-up of Jesus.
(Jesus ignores the people; stoops down and, with his finger, begins to write in the sand)

Shot Ten—Medium shot.
(camera moves to men's faces, to each man as he speaks)

Third Man: Aren't you going to say anything?

Fourth Man: I thought you knew all the answers.

Fifth Man: Come on, tell us what we should do.

Sixth Man: You know more about the Law than we Pharisees do; speak up.

First Man: What's the matter, cat got your tongue?

Second Man: If you are so wise, speak now.

Shot Eleven—Close-up, then pull back to medium-long shot of Jesus.
(Jesus slowly raises his head, looks at the men, then stands facing them; camera follows his action.)

Shot Twelve—Wide shot; Jesus facing men and woman.

Jesus: Whichever one of you has committed no sin may throw the first stone at her.
(Jesus stoops down again and continues to write in sand.)

Shot Thirteen—Long-range view.
(camera follows Jesus' action)

Shot Fourteen—Reaction shot; each character's response to Jesus' words.
(First man stoops and picks up a stone; begins to throw it, then stops, slowly lowers arm, lets stone fall to the ground, walks away. Camera follows, returns to focus on second man. Second man shakes head, strokes beard, walks away. Third man pounds fist into his hand in anger, seems puzzled about what to do, then walks away. Fourth man has been gathering stones; looks around, sees others are gone, turns and leaves, dropping stones as he goes. Fifth man has been holding the woman; drops her arm, spits at her feet, walks away. Sixth man looks around, very frightened, finds he is alone, turns and runs.)

Shot Fifteen—Long shot.
(wide shot showing Jesus kneeling and woman standing alone)

Shot Sixteen—Short-medium shot.

Jesus: Where are they? Is there no one left to condemn you?

Woman: No one, sir.

Jesus: Well, then, I do not condemn you either. Go, but do not sin again.

Shot Seventeen—Long shot; fade out.
(camera moves farther and farther away from scene)

SCENE III

Shot Eighteen—Close-up of interior; back to narrator.

Narrator: Once again the enemies of Jesus have failed to catch him in a false teaching. But the displeasure of his enemies increases more and more, and they are beginning to plan and plot to get rid of Jesus.

CHAPTER SEVEN

When I was growing up in a small southern town, Christmas in the church school always meant a tableau or pageant. It was years before I knew there was any other possible way to celebrate Christmas in the church school. One year the big picture frame would be hauled out of the church storeroom and placed on the stage. That was the year of the tableau. The next year the entire church school would be lined up for the pageant: Primary children—angels; Intermediate children—shepherds; Junior boys—wisemen; some older boy and girl as Mary and Joseph. And so it went, year after year, the simple Christmas story told in bathrobes and bedsheets.

Tableaus and pageants are less popular now, and we have wisely learned that these are only two methods of drama among many. However, there are still possibilities for their use if we remember that pageants are a spectacular rather than an educational form of drama, and tableaus serve the purpose of aesthetic entertainment rather than dramatic.

SEVENTEENTH WAY . . . TABLEAU

A tableau is a dramatic scene which is both silent and motionless. Two or more players freeze in an interesting pose for a few seconds, like a living picture. A frame or draperies should enclose the grouping. There should be some means to conclude the picture after a few seconds. If it is on a stage, the curtains can be drawn. If this is impossible, two students can raise and lower a sheet in front of the performers. Meanwhile the next picture or tableau is forming in the frame. It is a good idea to plan a number of different tableaus to be presented one after the other, if you are planning a stage presentation.

One advantage of the tableau is that you can work out your scenes to include everyone in your class. Perhaps you have students who prefer technical skills to picture posing. They can be responsible for constructing the frame or working out special lighting or appropriate recorded music. The use of color in costumes, lighting, and the grouping of the figures are the keys to a successful tableau.

The Saga of the Bible

The purpose of this tableau is to illustrate in visual form the history of the development of the Bible. This tableau includes seven scenes and presents a number of different historical periods. It could offer a colorful variety of costumes and scenes. Suggestions for costumes or picture poses are not included here.

Maximum learning will take place as students research their own costumes and plan their own scenes. This tableau could culminate a study of the history of the Bible, or it could actually *be* the study.

The Tableau

Narrator: The saga of the Bible spans many thousands of years, and the life, work, and death of many people. In the beginning God wanted to be known. People who were responsive came to understand what God was showing them in nature, in their lives, and in the lives of others. Before there was a written language, stories were memorized and faithfully repeated from one generation to the next.

Tableau 1—Scene of ancient people seated around a campfire

Narrator: The story of Creation and the beginning of life was told here. As the generations passed, the Great Flood and the story of Noah were told.
(curtain—music to cover changing of tableau, perhaps a hymn such as ''The Bible Is a Treasure Book'')

Tableau 2—Moses and the early Hebrews with stone tablets

Narrator: Out of the telling there gradually came to be writings. Perhaps these writings were first made on stones as reminders or monuments. When God made a covenant with the Hebrew people at Mount Sinai, the Ten Commandments were inscribed on stone tablets and placed in the sacred Ark of the Covenant.
(curtain—music)

Tableau 3—Group reading from scrolls

Narrator: The writings were later prepared on scrolls. There gradually came to be a body of sacred literature made up of the Law, the Prophets, and the Writings—the Old Testament. In the writings of the Old Testament was an expectation of a coming Messiah. In Jesus, the Messiah arrived, bringing a New Covenant with God. The story of Jesus' life and the early church, and the letters of his followers make up the New Testament.
(curtain—music)

Tableau 4—Monks copying Scripture

Narrator: As the Christian church grew, monasteries were established, where devoted monks gave their whole lives to carefully copying the precious Scriptures.
(curtain—music)

Tableau 5—Caedmon singing to farmers

Narrator: For many years after the writing of the Bible was completed, few people knew how to read. A laborer named Caedmon is said to have produced the first bit of English literature by singing some paraphrases of the Bible in the Anglo-Saxon dialect.
(curtain—music)

Tableau 6—People reading hardback Bibles

Narrator: Today there are many translations of the Bible in English. Some people think one translation is more clear than another. Each translation was made by a devoted and careful scholar.
(curtain—music)

Tableau 7—People from different countries

Narrator: The number of languages into which the Bible is translated continues to grow. The saga of the Bible is not complete. It continues to speak of God's purposes for the present and the future.

(curtain—music)

EIGHTEENTH WAY . . . PAGEANT

A pageant is an elaborate production. We usually think of a pageant as including a large number of people, music, and color. Several ages and subjects are drawn together, with drama the means of uniting them. A pageant offers the opportunity for a large group project with creative possibilities for many—costumes, stage properties, preparation.

A disadvantage of pageants in Christian education is that the final production sometimes becomes the most important thing; the creative aspects may be lost in the search for effect. We get caught up in bringing off a "great show." Rehearsals become a time of strain and drill, and the individual child may be sacrificed to perfection and detail. We become hassled over a striving for perfection against time and may end up with unhappy results.

Weighing against these negative aspects is a positive one. On special occasions in our church, such as the great festivals of Christmas and Easter or a historical event in our local church history, we want an extraordinary way to express our feelings. A pageant fits this need.

With proper organization and an awareness of the dangers, even an elaborate pageant can offer great joy to all.

The following Christmas pageant seeks to recognize the mobility of families and individuals in our time and the Christmas loneliness this mobility can bring. It uses a number of acting methods already mentioned in this book. It is suggested that the entire elementary department of your church school put on this pageant for the congregation. The work can be divided among a number of leaders. You will need a director for the speaking choir, the singing choir, and the pantomime choir, and also someone to organize and supervise the making of the friendship candle. These groups can work separately. If this method is followed there need not be more than one or two full rehearsals when the leader and Bible readers and organist are needed.

Christmas Makes Us One

A Christmas Program for the Entire Congregation

Included are: Speaking choir (suggested ages 8–10)
Singing choir (suggested ages 11–12)
Pantomime choir (suggested ages 5–7)

There should be one large friendship candle on a center table. Have the children gather candle stubs from the entire neighborhood and community. Melt all the colored candles together and pour into a large carton (large potato chip cartons work well), insert a wick, and allow to mold and cool. Save the white candle stubs for icing the candle. Melt these and whip with an egg beater until fluffy. When the candle is cool, remove the carton and ice the candle with the whipped white wax. A regular large candle can be used, but it will have more meaning for this program if the candle is made from the contributions of members of the congregation and neighborhood.

Instructions for Part 1:

The speaking choir should be arranged with boys on one side and girls on the other. There are four solo speaking parts. Solo 1 and Solo 2 should be good readers with voices that carry. Solo 3 is Oliver Cromwell and has only one solo line. Solo 4 is the town crier and should have a loud voice. Interpretation suggestions are included, but do not feel you must follow these closely. Be creative.

Part 1

Leader: It is Christmas in Idaho and Maine, in Florida and North Dakota. All across our land it is Christmas. Though our traditions and customs are different there is something about Christmas that makes us one. Just as shepherds came from their rural background, and wisemen from their learned citadels, so we come from many parts of the country to one celebration—to one manger—to Christmas.

Where are our Christmas pilgrims from? Are there those in the audience [or congregation] whose place of birth is the eastern part of our country? Will you stand to be recognized?
(let people stand, introduce themselves and give their state of birth)
When our ancestors first landed on the rocky coast of that part of our country, Christmas was celebrated quite differently from the way it is today. Our speaking choir will tell us about it.
(choir faces audience and speaks in a "once upon a time" voice; soloists speak from their places within the choir)

Solo 1:   The year is 1642.

Solo 2:   The place is New England.

All: We are pilgrim children.

Solo 1:   Oliver Cromwell is head of the Puritan government, and he has just announced:

Solo 3:   There will be no Christmas celebration this year!

Girls: *(facing the boys)* No Christmas celebration?

Boys: *(facing the girls, shaking their heads sadly)* Nothing at all.

Solo 2:   The pilgrims thought Christmas was rowdy and pagan.

All: *(facing the audience)* Even the town crier went about shouting:

Solo 4:   No Christmas! No Christmas!

Girls: *(to boys)* Mother says we must be pious.

Boys: *(to girls)* Father says we must be brave.

Boys: *(to audience)* For we have lands to conquer.

Girls: *(to audience)* And we have souls to save.

Solo 1:	For 22 years from the day they first landed on Plymouth Rock, there was no Christmas celebration in New England.
Girls:	*(sadly)* No presents.
Boys:	No cakes and cookies.
Girls:	No Christmas stockings.
Boys:	No Santa Claus.
Boys:	*(to audience)* People worked as usual.
Girls:	*(to audience)* Anyone caught lighting a Christmas candle was punished.
All:	And the town crier went around shouting:
Solo 4:	No Christmas! No Christmas!
Boys:	For our parents were busy and strong-minded and serious.
Girls:	They did not hold with glee.
All:	And they called a merry person a sinner.
Boys:	No one said "Merry Christmas!"
Girls:	Or even "Alleluia!"
All:	And the town crier kept shouting:
Solo 4:	No Christmas! No Christmas!
Girls:	We had clothes to wash,
Boys:	and powder horns to fill,
Girls:	and floors to scrub,
Boys:	and food to kill,
All:	and nothing but sermons at Sunday meetings.
Solo 1:	So Christmas began in America with fasts instead of feasts, and solemn faces rather than joyful looks.
Solo 2:	But slowly, as life became easier,
Girls:	*(begin crescendo in reading)* candles appeared.

Boys: Feasting began.

All: The town crier was silent.

Solo 1: And 200 years later there were carols, and in that very same part of the country, our favorite American Christmas carol was written.

Solo 2: Join us as we sing "O Little Town of Bethlehem," written in the city of Philadelphia.

Instructions for Part 2:

In this portion of the program a choir will sing three Christmas carols, and three announcers will set the mood for each number. If you are unable to locate the music for these carols, or if you prefer others, substitutions may be made—suggested for the English carol: "God Rest You Merry, Gentlemen," "The Boar's Head Carol," "Good King Wenceslas," "Here We Come A-caroling"; for the French carol: "Angels We Have Heard on High," "The First Noel," "Shepherds, Shake Off Your Drowsy Sleep," "O Holy Night"; for the spiritual: "Rise Up, Shepherd," "Follow," "Wasn't That a Mighty Day," "Poor Little Jesus."

Part 2

Leader: Do we have Christmas pilgrims from the southern part of our country?
(let them stand, introduce themselves and give their state of birth)
Christmas began in the South in a number of places and in a number of ways. Our singing choir will tell us about it.

First Announcer: When our ancestors came from England to Virginia they brought many of their English customs with them. Of course their favorite carols were English. As we sing "Deck the Halls" for you, try to picture this scene in your mind. A lovely manor house—friends and relatives gathered around—a Yule log burning in the open fireplace—the windows, doors, and mantels decked with holly, ivy, and mistletoe—a table groaning with turkey, hams, apples, and flaming pudding. After dancing the reel to the fiddler's tune, the whole group would gather to sing such carols as these:

(choir sings "Deck the Halls")

Traditional   *Old Welsh Air*

Deck the halls with boughs of holly,
Fa la la la la, la la la la.
'Tis the season to be jolly,
Fa la la la la, la la la la.
Don we now our gay apparel,
Fa la la, la la la, la la la.
Troll the ancient Yuletide carol,
Fa la la la la, la la la la.

See the blazing Yule before us,
Fa la la la, la la la la la.
Strike the harp and join the chorus,

Fa la la la la, la la la la.
Follow me in merry measure,
Fa la la, la la la, la la la.
While I tell of Yuletide's treasure.
Fa la la la la, la la la la.

Fast away the old year passes,
Fa la la la la, la la la la.
Hail the new, ye lads and lasses,
Fa la la la la, la la la la.
Sing we joyous all together,
Fa la la, la la la, la la la.
Heedless of the wind and weather.
Fa la la la la, la la la la.

Second Announcer: Meanwhile in New Orleans, Christmas celebrations came from a French background. Change the image in your mind now and try to imagine tall white houses with wrought-iron balconies. Imagine the smell of Creole food cooking in the kitchens. Christmas in New Orleans was a week-long celebration of balls and banquets. Children received gifts twice—on Christmas morning and on New Year's morning. Picture, in a prominent place in the household, a crèche with Mary, Joseph, and baby Jesus. The French people celebrated with quite elaborate festivities. At midnight on Christmas Eve, everyone lighted a torch or candle and joined the Christmas procession. Picture this as we sing "Bring a Torch, Jeannette, Isabella!"

Traditional   *Traditional*

Bring a torch, Jeannette, Isabella!
Bring a torch, to the cradle run!
It is Jesus, good folk of the village,
Christ is born and Mary's calling.
Ah! ah! Beautiful is the mother;
Ah! ah! Beautiful is her Son!!

It is wrong when the Child is sleeping,
It is wrong to talk so loud;
Silence, all, as you gather round,
Lest your noise should waken Jesus;
Hush! Hush! See how the Child is sleeping;
Hush! Hush! See how fast He sleeps!

Softly to the little stable,
Softly for a moment come;
Look and see how charming is Jesus,
How He is white, His cheeks are rosy!
Hush! Hush! See how the Child is sleeping;
Hush! Hush! See how He smiles in dreams!

Third Announcer: Another tradition arose early in the South. From cabins behind the "big house," Negro servants were creating their own Christmas customs and celebrations. The custom of Christmas Gif' was a surprise game played by the slaves on Christmas Day. Two people meeting for the first time that day would rush to be the first to call out "Christmas Gif'"! The loser would forfeit a simple present—a few nuts or a Christmas cupcake. The giving was heartwarming to a people with so little they could, with dignity, share with others.

Spirituals capture this same simplicity and add a new dimension to the wonder and beauty of the Christmas story. We will sing for you, "Go Tell It on the Mountain."

Spiritual

When I was a learner, I sought both night and day;
I asked the Lord to aid me and He showed me the way.
Go, tell it on the mountain,
Over the hills an' everywhere,
Go, tell it on the mountain,
Our Jesus Christ is born.

He made me a watchman upon the city wall;
An' if I am a Christian I am the least of all.
Go, tell it on the mountain,
Over the hills an' everywhere,
Go, tell it on the mountain,
Our Jesus Christ is born.

Instructions for Part 3:

This portion of the program is a simple pantomime. Explain to the children that they are shepherds who have just heard the news of the birth of Jesus and have left their sheep and gone to Bethlehem to look for the new Baby. They will knock on doors in the village, seeking Jesus. One child plays the part of the Devil, who tries to keep the shepherds away. That child should come in first and crouch along the path the procession of shepherds will be following. At the appropriate time the Devil jumps out and blocks the shepherds' way. The leader of the procession of shepherds stops momentarily, then continues, walking around and ignoring the Devil. The others follow this example. The Devil crouches back to earth. The Reader should be an adult who can fit the reading to the children's action, and the procession of shepherds should be led by a dependable, able child skilled in pantomime. Simple shepherd costumes will add to the impact of this portion of the program.

Part 3

Leader: Do we have Christmas pilgrims with us tonight from the West?
(let them stand, introduce themselves and give their state of birth)

Reader: Even before the pilgrims were frowning on Christmas celebrations, the earliest settlers in California and old New Mexico were observing Christmas with Spanish customs. If you had been a child in those days, you would have dressed as a shepherd or shepherdess and gone from house to house throughout your town, seeking the Babe of Bethlehem.
(children enter dressed as shepherds; some may carry a shepherd's crook; they process down the aisle and pantomime knocking on a series of doors)

Reader: Knocking on the doors of the town, they asked, "Where is the Christ Child? Where is the manger?"
(children pantomime asking these questions—or actually ask them; at each door they shake their heads "no" and continue the procession; the children can circle the church or fellowship hall)

Reader: In one version of this ancient Spanish play, the Devil tries to keep the shepherds from going to Bethlehem.
(one child pantomiming the Devil jumps in front of the procession and tries to block the way; procession stops for a moment)

Reader: But the Devil is unsuccessful and the shepherds always win out.
(children continue, walking around the Devil)

Reader: At last they reach the manger.
(procession arrives at front of church or fellowship hall)

Reader: This time they enter and kneel before the Christ Child.
(procession kneels)

Reader: When this play was enacted by early settlers, the children arrived at last at the house of their friends. The host and hostess took them in and festival time began. There were games and presents and piñatas.
(pantomime choir rises and faces audience)

Reader: A Christmas carol that captures this feeling of the shepherd's joyful procession is "Angels We Have Heard on High." The joyousness of the rhythm brings to mind childrens' voices, clear and melodious. Let's all join in singing this carol.

Instructions for Part 4:

Four readers from the speaking choir come forward and take their places in the front of the room. They may be dressed in western-type clothes.

Part 4

Leader: Do we have Christmas pilgrims from the Midwest?
(let them stand, introduce themselves and give their state of birth)
Though we think of early frontier life as being rough and lonely, Christmas had a special place there, too. What might it have been like for pioneer children in the early Midwest?

Solo 1:   We began to get excited several weeks before Christmas.

Solo 2:   I went with Dad in the wagon to town for luxuries like sugar and coffee.

Solo 3:   I helped Mother get the cabin ready for neighbors who came from half a state away.

Solo 4:   I helped with the cooking. I gathered the nuts and made the mince pies and the clove-scented apple dumplings.

Solo 1:   What a happy time it is!

Solo 2:   Once I was allowed to go on an all-night wild-turkey shoot.

Solo 3:   I like the candy-pulls best.

Solo 4:   I like the music, when everyone dances to the fiddle and harmonica.

Solo 1:   Our presents are wooden dolls and rifles

Solo 2:   carved by our father.

Solo 3:   Or clothing made by our mother.

Solo 4:   And sometimes we have a Christmas tree with homemade decorations.

Solo 1:   And a wreath with a ribbon for the door.

Solo 2:   Christmas has two moods for us—a holy day and a holiday.

Solo 3:   We pray and dance.

Solo 4:   There is worship and festivity.

Solo 1:   And we remember it most as a family time.

Solo 2:   A hymn that captures our feeling of happiness is "Joy to the World."
        (entire congregation joins in singing)

Leader: America has been called a melting pot, and our various Christmas customs and traditions illustrate this. As our country grew and settlers came from all over the world, they brought with them their cherished Christmas celebrations—unique and special to them. I am sure all of you here have your favorite Christmas traditions. But now, our customs and traditions meet—here, symbolized by the friendship candle on the table. It was made from many candles—some of them yours. But now they are melted together to give us our Christmas light.
        (child comes forward and lights large candle)

Reader: Let us listen now to the Gospel records from three sections of the Eastern world. First, from Asia Minor:

**Reader
from Audience:**   *(reads Matthew 2:1-12)*

Reader: From Ephesus, written in the Greek language, we have this record:

**Reader
from Audience:**   *(reads Luke 2:1-20)*

Leader: And from Rome, to the Christians at Philippi, came this word:

**Reader
from Audience:**   *(reads Philippians 2:1-11)*

Leader: Across the years, across the miles, we come to celebrate Christmas. Though we have traveled many roads, our paths merge for a moment, and we become pilgrims together on the road to Bethlehem. And though our backgrounds are different, our purpose is similar. Christmas makes us one.

End the program with "Silent Night"; during the singing, members of the choir come forward single-file and light small candles at the large friendship candle. They may either form a circle around the friendship candle and remain until the hymn is concluded, or process from the church with their lighted candles.

NINETEENTH WAY . . . CHANCEL DRAMA

Probably the most widely used form of religious drama in the church is the chancel drama. Most churches, at one time or another, have produced a play in the chancel area or brought in a professional group to present such a play. This can be a very meaningful experience for a congregation. There is no more dynamic way of communicating ideas than through a dramatic presentation by an effective drama group with a religious orientation.

If your group is interested in presenting a chancel drama, there are several items to consider before you begin.

First, who will be putting on the play? A serious chancel drama should not be attempted with children. This is a project for adults and older youth.

Second, look at the play itself. Recognize the importance of standards and resist the temptation to use easy, superficial plays. They have no place in the chancel of the church! The play may be biblically oriented or it may deal with serious contemporary themes and issues. Drama for the chancel should be profound. It should help us discover something about ourselves and our relationship to God. Some professional dramas can do this effectively. On the other hand, a church has the opportunity to do plays which would never be effective on the commercial stage. Some good plays are being written strictly for chancel presentation.

Having selected the appropriate play, look next at your physical arrangements. By presenting a serious drama within the church, the physical surroundings add a psychological dimension. People are ready to listen to a serious subject; the general atmosphere sets a receptive mood. An important fact to remember is this: A place of worship should not be made into a theater in order to present a play. Chancel drama does not achieve its purpose if the area must be so completely rearranged that the worship atmosphere is eliminated. If you have to build sets that change your entire chancel area, forget it and present it in your fellowship hall or choose another play.

Most plays will need some adjustment for your particular church. Check these physical arrangements for a more effective performance:

1. What about sounds? Most churches do not have the acoustics of a theater and this can present a problem.
2. What about sight? Is there room for actors to move freely in full view of the congregation?
3. What about entrances and exits? You will not have the curtain of a theater, and your entrances may be some distance from the area of the play. Some plays may have to be reworked, with actors entering from the audience.
4. What about audience comfort? Pews are not the most comfortable seating for long plays. You might wish to consider an extra intermission.
5. What about musical background? If your church has an organ, it can be used effectively to create moods, punctuate climaxes, and fill in between scenes.

6. What about the lectern and pulpit? Can you tie these into your production, perhaps to be used by a narrator or reader, or even to effectively set off long monologues?

There are two considerations in choosing a chancel drama: Is the play suitable? Is it adaptable to your chancel?

One final word of caution. Copyright laws are strict, and most plays can be used only upon payment of a royalty.

Drama in the chancel need not be confined to plays. Other dramatic forms can be integrated readily into an actual worship service. From its onset, Christian liturgy has contained a dramatic element—"The Word enacted." Our sacraments all contain drama; some other examples:

1. The Scripture lesson can be read in playscript form. The book of Job is particularly suited to this.
2. Little solo dramas or monologues, with a biblical character speaking thoughts and reactions to certain situations, are effective for congregational understanding and interest.
3. Dialogue sermons between two or more persons are suitable in some situations.
4. Responsive readings that involve the congregation are a form of drama.
5. A short chancel drama can take the place of the sermon in a service.

C H A P T E R   E I G H T

Games, simulations, clowning, and the writing of your own play—all are forms of drama. The approaches we have looked at so far have been used to study Scripture actually and critically. It is time to consider studying imaginatively and playfully. We know that children learn through play and that play of the imagination is equally important for adults. Simulations, games, and clowning are designed to help us *feel* the biblical events, sense the characters' feelings, and give us a deeper understanding of the meaning and power of the biblical message. Though there is an element of play in all drama, the following approaches go a step farther.

TWENTIETH WAY . . . THEATER GAMES

Certain schools of drama use the theater-game approach to teach and sensitize their actors. Their purpose is to develop sensitivity, make students aware of sensory feelings, and give creative vent to imaginations. These are also the goals we seek to teach, but our purpose is to apply them to Bible stories so that we may appreciate and experience a moment from Bible history in a unique way.

Four Games to Teach the Story of Joseph
(BASED ON GENESIS 37:3-28)

These games introduce the story of Joseph. The purpose is not to introduce the facts, but rather the feelings, the color, the objects, and the conflicts behind the facts.

Game 1—Identify the Objects

Players stand in a circle with their hands behind their backs. Objects are passed from one player to another. By touch, the students try to identify each object. The teacher calls on various members of the class to guess what each is. Use these objects:

A coin (quarter or half dollar)
A doll's coat
A stalk of wheat or other grain
A Styrofoam star
A toy wooly lamb

After the game, have the students read Genesis 37:3-28 and find the places where each object relates to the story.

Game 2—Relating an Incident

Choose two players to come before the class. "A" is to relate the story from Genesis 37:18,19 in the first person, in as simple a way as possible. "B" then repeats the story, adding colors.

For Example: "A" might say, "I was going to see my brothers in the field. I was wearing my new coat. My brothers saw me coming." "B" might say, "I was walking through the fresh green pastures looking for my tanned, shepherd brothers and their wooly brown and black sheep. I was wearing a coat of yellow, red, green, blue, and lavender. My brothers saw the vividly colored coat from afar."

Other teams of two might want to try the same passage. Or you might pick other passages from Genesis 37:3-28. The point of this game is to make the story more real to the students, to help them create in their minds a picture full of color and action.

Game 3—Conflict Tug of War

The point of this game is to help the students feel the tension between Joseph and his brothers in a very physical way.

You will need a strong rope and two players, one to represent Joseph and one to represent a brother. Have the students play a real tug-of-war game, attempting to pull the opponent over the center line. Let a number of students do this, and then discuss the feelings the players had. Can they relate those feelings to the conflict and tension felt between Joseph and his brothers? Reread the Bible story to discover the causes of that tension.

Game 4—Silent Scream

The point of this game is to help the students identify with the fear and horror Joseph would have felt when he was in the pit.

Ask the students to scream without making a sound. Coach them to scream with their faces, their bodies, their mouths. While they are responding, call out, "Scream out loud!" The sound should be deafening, and the impact of the reality of Joseph's fear should be dramatic.

Conclusion:

We have had an introduction today to Joseph—the feelings and surroundings that affected his entire life. As we continue our study we will discover the consequences of those feelings.

Do not underrate this experience. Though the students may not seem to be learning anything, all these experiences will come back to them vividly during the week and for many weeks. As a student absorbs the experience, it will take on more meaning. This will not be a lesson quickly forgotten.

TWENTY-FIRST WAY . . . SIMULATION GAMES

In a simulation game, an event is reenacted to bring certain features of that event vividly before us. Simulation is closely related to drama. In drama we act out an event to feature some fundamental truth. In biblical simulations, we act out a situation in order to perceive and explore the truth that is there. For example, in a simulation of Moses and the Israelites during the Exodus, we try to simulate, so that we may understand, the hunger, the apprehension, the tediousness, the doubts; and we find within ourselves some of the same reactions the Israelites experienced. Simulations are also like games. We take a game approach with rules and a predetermined goal. But the point of simulations is not to win, but to appreciate an event in order to learn from it. Later reflection on the game and the feelings it aroused is very important.

Most simulations, by their nature, take a long time to play, so this is an excellent activity for weekend retreats with youths or adults.

Here is a short simulation game for use during your church school session. Its purpose is to introduce simulation games to your class and illustrate a unique way to study the Bible story of the bridesmaids at the wedding (Matt. 25:1-13). This game is recommended for a small class of 10- and 11-year-olds. You will need:

A cake

A birthday candle and matches for each student playing the game

A timer that will go off after one minute

Ten slips of paper—9 saying No, 1 saying Yes

Rules:

Students are seated around the cake. Each student is given a birthday candle and matches. When the guest of honor arrives, every candle should be blazing on the cake. But we don't know when the guest will arrive! A pile of slips of paper is placed close to the players—nine slips of paper contain the word *no;* one slip of paper contains the word *yes.* Shuffle the slips so that the order is unknown. Clockwise around the circle, players will choose a slip of paper.

The teacher says, "I hear someone coming. Is it the guest of honor?" Each student then decides whether or not to light a candle. Players may elect not to light their candles. A player chooses a slip of paper to answer the question. If No, the candles that are lit must burn for one minute. Check with the timer.

The teacher asks the question again and the procedure is repeated. When a candle is burned out, a student is out of the game.

If the answer Yes is turned up, students whose candles are burning are the winners of the game and are given a piece of the cake. Losers do not receive any.

After the game read the Bible story from Matthew 25:1-13. Explain that weddings in Jesus' day had customs different from ours. A whole week of parties and merrymaking began with a joyful wedding feast. The bride chose ten girls her own age to help her prepare for the wedding. They had to be ready by evening, when the groom and his friends came to fetch the bride. Then they would all make their way to the house of the groom for the grand wedding feast.

Because the procession took place in the evening, lights were needed to show the way, and it was the duty of the bridesmaids to provide those lights. They used small clay lamps which burned olive oil. It was very important that the bridesmaids light the procession.

Since ancient people told time by the sun, rather than by clocks as we do, it was difficult to know the exact time the groom would arrive. As they waited, some of the bridesmaids used up their oil. Five sensible girls had come prepared with extra oil and were ready when the procession arrived. But the other girls ran off to find more oil and missed the procession. When they finally arrived at the groom's house, the feast was in progress. They banged on the door to be let in, but it was thought that all the guests were present, so they were sent away.

Can we appreciate how the bridesmaids must have felt? What were your feelings as losers, when you were not given any cake? Why do you think Jesus told this story?

After the discussion you may wish to conclude with something like this: Jesus told this story to illustrate that he had come to make known the love of God for all people. He invited all to come and enter the family of God. Some people are careless about the invitation, like the five foolish bridesmaids. They do not think about it seriously. They do not prepare themselves. They are in danger of being shut out of the kingdom of God, just as the careless girls were shut out of the wedding feast.

TWENTY-SECOND WAY . . . FOOT DRAMA

Using a part of the body as the actor can be a unique and fun way to dramatize Scripture. Hands can be actors, as well as individual fingers. Even eyebrows can give Yes and No responses to a story. For a really different approach, try using feet as actors. This is especially fun for teenagers.

Instructions:

The actors are a person's feet, decorated with felt-tip pens to make faces—eyes on the soles of feet, mouth on the heel, and nose somewhere in between. This play uses two feet (two actors).

The stage is a large cardboard box. One side is open. Cut two holes in the other side for the feet to stick through. Make the holes large enough to allow movement of the feet and close enough for feet to interact with each other. A person sits or lies on the floor and sticks the foot actors through the holes. Feet, of course, cannot do many movements, but they can bob up and down and from side to side. The toes can serve as hands for using props. A narrator reads the parts.

Jesus Teaches About Revenge

(BASED ON MATTHEW 5)

Narrator:	You have heard that it was said, "An eye for an eye, and a tooth for a tooth." *(two foot actors appear and bump each other—first one, then the other, in identical manner)*
Foot Actor One:	*(pokes toe in "eye" of Foot Actor Two)*
Foot Actor Two:	*(does the same to Foot Actor One)*
Foot Actor One:	*(bops Foot Actor Two in mouth)*
Foot Actor Two:	*(repeats same action on Foot Actor One)* *(other actions of beating on each other in the manner of Punch and Judy shows may be performed; be certain each action done by one foot actor is repeated by the second foot actor)*
Narrator:	But now I tell you; do not take revenge on someone who wrongs you. If anyone slaps you on the right cheek, let him slap your left cheek too.
Foot Actor One:	*(gives Foot Actor Two a mighty slap on one side of face)*
Foot Actor Two:	*(staggers from blow, weaves from side-to-side; then slowly, turns to Foot Actor One and offers other side of face)* *(feet exit out of sight)*
Narrator:	If someone takes you to court to sue you for your shirt, let him have your coat as well. *(feet appear on stage)*
Foot Actor One:	*(has a hat on toes and a cape hanging behind)*

Foot Actor Two:	*(removes cape from Foot Actor One, picking it off with toes)*
Foot Actor One:	*(bends over, offering hat to Foot Actor Two)* *(feet exit)*
Narrator:	And if one of the occupation troops forces you to carry his pack one mile, carry it two miles. *(feet appear on stage)*
Foot Actor One:	*(carries a bag with toes; drops it in front of Foot Actor Two)*
Foot Actor Two:	*(turns and looks at Foot Actor One; then bends and picks bag up with toes)*
Both Actors:	*(move up and down as though walking; they stop)*
Foot Actor One:	*(looks at Foot Actor Two)*
Foot Actor Two:	*(shakes head no)* *(the two foot actors continue walking motion, Foot Actor Two still carrying the load)*
Narrator:	You must be perfect, just as your Father in heaven is perfect.

TWENTY-THIRD WAY . . . A STRING-TRICK STORY

Children, pieces of string, and fingers on which to weave create a delightful way to tell the Christmas episode "The Holy Family Escapes," based on Matthew 2.

String was used in an ancient method of storytelling. The storyteller would use loops of string to capture the attention of the audience and make the story come alive.

Many elementary children play Cat's Cradle or Kitten's Whiskers, weaving string patterns with their fingers. The children can learn to create a similar string pattern and become tellers of this Christmas story themselves.

Instructions:

—Practice the string trick until you can do it perfectly.
—Tell the story to the children, using the movements of the string.
—Teach the children how to do "The Holy Family Escapes" string trick.
—Let them take turns telling you the story.
—There are several educational values in using this method: repetition for emphasis, whole-body learning, and fun!

You will need a piece of string for each child in the class. Nylon cord works best, but butcher's string or macrame cord can be used. Each string should be 2 meters long. The string can be either tied or, if using nylon cord, melted together to form a loop of one meter.

How to Do the String Trick:

Step 1:	Hang the string loop over the fingers and thumb of your left hand.
Step 2:	Put your right hand into the hanging loop. Use your right index finger like a hook to take hold of the string that crosses between your left thumb and index finger. With your

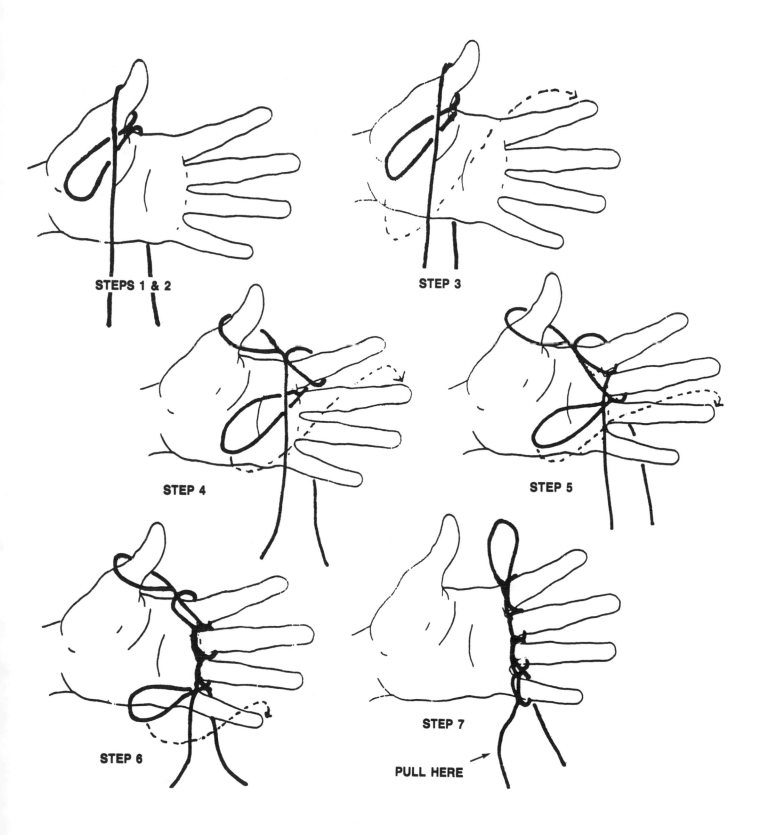

STEPS 1 & 2

STEP 3

STEP 4

STEP 5

STEP 6

STEP 7

PULL HERE

right index finger, pull out a short loop in this string. Pull the loop out *under* the string that hangs over your left thumb. Keep the loop straight.

Step 3:   Hold this loop with your right index finger and thumb and give it half a twist clockwise. Put this loop on your left index finger and pull on the hanging loop to tighten; the strings. (This process will be repeated on the rest of your fingers. Keep one string across your palm and one hanging down the back. Continue to use the right index finger as a hook, working under the string that hangs across your palm. Don't forget to add the twist each time.)

Step 4:   Pull out a loop in the back string between your index finger and middle finger. As before, pull it out under the string that hangs across your palm, give it a half twist clockwise, and put it on your middle finger. Tighten the strings.

Step 5:   Pull out a loop between your middle finger and fourth finger, give it a half twist clockwise, and put it on your fourth finger. Tighten the strings.

Step 6:   Pull out a loop between your fourth finger and little finger, give it half a twist clockwise, and put it on your little finger. Tighten the strings.

Step 7:   Take the loop off your thumb. Pull the front string of the hanging loop.

The Holy Family Escapes
(BASED ON MATTHEW 2)

You all know the story of the three wise men who came to worship the baby Jesus. They traveled many miles, following the star. Often they stopped along the way, seeking, searching. They even stopped at the palace of King Herod to inquire where the new baby would be found. But the king did not know.

At last the star stopped over the stable in Bethlehem. The wise men entered, knelt before the baby, and gave him the rich treasures they had brought from their homelands.

But God spoke to the wise men in a dream one night while they were in Bethlehem and warned them not to tell Herod they had found Jesus. King Herod was frightened that a new king might take over this throne, and he plotted to kill Jesus as soon as he was found.

Not long afterward an angel said to Joseph in a dream, "Arise, take the young child and his mother and flee into Egypt, for Herod will search for Jesus and try to kill him." Joseph got up while it was still dark.

Begin String Trick

Step 1—Hang the string loop over the fingers.
    Quietly and carefully, Joseph gathered all his belongings together.

Step 2—Pull out loop between thumb and fingers.
    He did not forget to include the bag of gold from the first wise man.

Step 3—Put loop over left index finger.
    Then he carefully loaded the casket containing the frankincense, brought by the second wise man.

Step 4—Put loop over middle finger.
   He tied on the donkey the container of myrrh brought by the third wise man.

Step 5—Put loop over fourth finger.
   Then he quietly awakened Mary. She rose, carrying the sleeping Jesus.

Step 6—Put loop over little finger.
   Now all was in readiness for their journey to Egypt. When Herod realized that the wise men had not returned to tell him where to find Jesus, he was furious. He gathered his troops and stormed away.

Step 7—Pull the front string.
   But the family escaped with all its belongings, to the land of Egypt.

TWENTY-FOURTH WAY . . . CLOWNING

Clown ministry is an exciting form of drama to use in teaching the Bible. Clowns suggest fun and childlikeness and vulnerability and instant communication. A clown expresses things nonverbally and in an exaggerated way. This can give new insight into a Bible story. It is a way of playing with Scripture. It affirms that humor is legitimate.

The following example is suggested for use in a youth Sunday school class or evening meeting. Usually face makeup and costumes are an important part of clown ministry. Because of the time frame of a structured class setting, they are not suggested here, but you may wish to expand this lesson to include them.

Step One—Ask the class, "What are some things a clown does?" and write the answers on the board. Suggest these ideas if the class has not come up with them:
   —Clowns act joyful and foolish
   —Clowns act in loving ways
   —Clowns take everyday objects and transform them into something else.
   —Clowns make us laugh because everything they do goes wrong.
   —Clowns point out injustice, sadness, sorrow, and grief, so that we can deal with them.
   —Clowns help us laugh at ourselves.
   —Clowns help us see it is good to be fools for Christ.

Step Two—Warm up. Have on hand some toys for blowing bubbles, balloons (the long kind that can be made into animals), crepe-paper streamers on dowels, musical instruments, oversized flowers, colorful wigs, big floppy shoes. The teacher instructs the class to use the "What Clowns Do" list on the board and act like clowns. Give the students a few minutes to freely, **silently**, interact with the objects. There is no set routine. This is a time to let the class loosen up, have fun, express joy and happiness and foolishness.

Step Three—When students seem free and relaxed, ask the group to sit in a circle. Explain that there are three basic types of clowns:
   1. The white-face clown is bouncy, happy, playful, silly
   2. The sad-faced hobo clown is droopy and unhappy
   3. The Auguste clown is a klutz, always tripping, falling down, breaking things

Have on hand a package of figs. Give one to each student. Acting as one of the three types of clowns, each student is to pantomime some action with the fig. The student can eat it (sad or happy), turn it into a flower and smell it, transform it into a horn and toot it, keep dropping it, get it stuck on the fingers, whatever the imagination suggests.

Step Four—Divide the class into groups of three. Each group will read Luke 13:6-9, the parable of the unfruitful fig tree.

Step Five—Each group creates a charade of this parable without words, using clown techniques. First a group decides on the central point of the story. Each member of the group will be a character in the charade: the gardener, the fig tree, or the owner of the vineyard. Decide who will do each part and which character will be the clown. Will it be the gardener, who does everything wrong and keeps the tree from growing? Will it be the tree, too droopy to produce fruit? Will it be the owner of the vineyard, too carefree to care about the fig tree? Or is the gardener the carefree one and the owner the droopy one? The group chooses some variation, trying to stay true to the central meaning of the parable as the students understand it.

Step Six—Create props, costumes, settings from whatever is in the room, transforming it with imagination.

Step Seven—The fun part comes when each group presents its charade for the other students. The interpretation of this parable is often different with each group.

Step Eight—Following all the skits, the entire class discusses the parable. Which skit best captured the central meaning? What new insight into the parable did you receive as you watched the other skits?

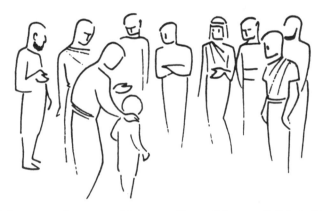

"Unless you change and become like children . . ." (Matt. 18:3)

TWENTY-FIFTH WAY . . . DRAMA FOR COGNITIVE LEARNING

The Bible is difficult for many children because the words used, the cultural references, the customs, are strange or even unknown. Not knowing the reference, a child may miss the main point of the passage. Often this study of references becomes boring for children. Drama can be a fun way to accomplish the same purpose. Following is a silly skit to explain the meaning of the word *millstone* as used by Jesus in Matthew 18:6.

This skit has two actors: Radio Announcer and You. The two students chosen to do this skit look over the part and then present it for the group.

The Skit

(*phone rings*)

You: Hello

Radio Announcer: Is this _____?

You: Yes it is.

Radio Announcer: Do you live at _____?

You: That's correct.

Radio Announcer: Congratulations: Your name was chosen at random from the telephone directory. If you can answer one question, you will win dinner for two at La Supreme Restaurant.

You: La Supreme Restaurant? Wow! That's great!

Radio Announcer: Are you ready?

You: I'm ready! I'm ready!

Radio Announcer: It's a biblical question. The answer to this question is an object with two parts.

You: Two parts! Two parts! Got it! Two parts . . . It's the Bible—Old and New Testament—two parts!

Radio Announcer: Wait—I haven't asked the question yet!

You: Oops, sorry.

Radio Announcer: Here it is. Now listen carefully. Jesus said, "It is better for a man to have _____ hung around his neck and be drowned in the sea than for him to cause one of these little ones to lose faith in me." What is the object?

You: Jesus said that, did he? It must be a two-part necklace.

Radio Announcer: No, I'm sorry.

You: Wait! Wait! Give me a hint.

Radio Announcer: Oh all right! A wooden shaft is fitted into this object and a donkey is yoked to it. The donkey goes round and round in a circle.

You: A donkey? Going round and round in a circle? What is this—a trick question? Is it a merry-go-round?

Radio Announcer: I'm sorry. I don't think you are going to get this at all. Here's one more hint. It was used in Jesus' day for making olive oil.

You:	Olive oil! I love it! I love olive oil!
Radio Announcer:	The answer is—a millstone.
You:	A millstone! I knew it! I knew it! I was just about to say it. One part is a round stone through which the olives are put, and then the heavy millstone is rolled round on its edge inside the trough.
Radio Announcer:	That's correct.
You:	And . . . and . . . the wooden shaft goes through the millstone, and the donkey turns the stone until the oil is forced out of the olives.
Radio Announcer:	Yes, but I am afraid your answer was too late.
You:	The Greek word used in the Bible (Matt. 18:6) literally means "a donkey millstone." I knew it! I knew it! I knew the answer.
Radio Announcer:	I am sorry!
You:	You mean I won't get my dinner for two? Can you at least tell me what they were serving?
Radio Announcer:	Olive souffle!

TWENTY-SIXTH WAY . . . WRITE YOUR OWN PLAY

Probably the most helpful play you can use in teaching church school is the one you write yourself. After having tried some of the experiences suggested in this book, your students should feel comfortable with movement, speech, and self-expression. The development of their imaginations should result in a flow of ideas. You are now ready to organize those ideas into a play.

Following are some steps to help guide you. The entire class should be involved in this process.
1. Choose a Bible story. A story that can be interpreted literally, rather than symbolically, will work best for your first attempt.
2. Decide what characters you will need.
3. Decide how many scenes there will be and write an outline of what will happen in these scenes.
4. Have some students act it out, making up words as they go along. Then decide with the class: What was good? What do we want to keep? What should we leave out? What could be improved?
5. Act out a revised version.
6. When you are satisfied with the scenes, write down the words in play form.
7. Decide on props, background, and costumes, if any.

You have written a play! Polish it up and perfect it. It may be performed, or the writing and creating of the play may be the entire learning experience.